hugo

in **3** MONTHS

ITALIAN

Milena Reynolds

A DORLING KINDERSLEY BOOK

LONDON, NEW YORK, MUNICH,
MELBOURNE, AND DELHI

This edition first published in Great Britain
in 2003 by Dorling Kindersley Limited,
80 Strand, London WC2R 0RL

First published in Great Britain by
Hugo's Language Books Limited

Copyright © 2003 Dorling Kindersley Limited
A Penguin Company
4 6 8 10 9 7 5 3

A CIP catalogue record is available from the British Library.
ISBN 1 40530 102 3

Hugo Italian in Three Months is also available in
a pack with three CDs, ISBN 0 7513 6992 6

Written by
Milena Reynolds
Lecturer in Italian
Morley College, London

Printed and bound in China by Leo Paper Product LTD

see our complete catalogue at
www.dk.com

Preface

This new edition of *Hugo Italian in Three Months* has been written for us by Milena Reynolds, whose experience in teaching her native tongue ranges from beginners to post graduate level. She has drawn on this expertise to produce a simple yet complete course for students aiming to acquire a good working knowledge of the language in a short time, and who will probably be working at home alone. The course also covers all the basic GCSE syllabus, both structural and communicative, and so could be used as a class textbook for that exam.

The book begins with a detailed study of pronunciation (our 'imitated' system will help you through the early stages). The rest of the course is divided into ten parts, each of which should take roughly a week to complete – so even if you proceed slightly slower than expected, you will still finish the course inside three months. Each part has a main theme divided into three or four related topics with dialogues, through which the grammar is presented concisely and clearly, with plenty of examples and exercises. This course maintains the Hugo principle of teaching only what is really essential for a firm grasp of practical, up-to-date Italian. Using the book together with our CDs is an ideal combination and provides a further dimension to your studies.

Ideally you should spend about an hour a day on the course (maybe a little less if you don't have the CDs), although there is no hard and fast rule on this. Do as much as you feel capable of doing; it is much better to learn a little at a time, and to learn that thoroughly. At the beginning of each day's session, spend ten minutes recalling what you learned the day before. When you read a conversation, say it out loud if possible (listen to the CD and see how closely you can imitate the native speakers).

Study each rule or numbered section carefully and re-read it to ensure that you have fully understood the grammar and examples given. Then revisit the preceding conversation and note how it embodies the constructions explained in the numbered sections. Next do the associated exercises. Try to understand rather than memorise; if you have understood, the exercises will ensure that you remember the rules through applying them.

When the course is completed, you should have a very good knowledge of Italian – more than sufficient for general holiday or business use, and enough to lead quickly into an examination syllabus if required. We hope you will enjoy *Hugo Italian in Three Months*, and wish you success with your studies.

Contents

Pronunciation

Before you start the first chapter, read the following rules on pronunciation. If you use the CDs, read the words and sentences while you listen. Italian pronunciation is easy and once you have mastered those sounds which are different from English you will find that you can pronounce the printed words quite easily. When reading, follow the basic rules of our imitated pronunciation given below.

THE IMITATED PRONUNCIATION

For a while we give the imitated pronunciation for each new word as it occurs in the text or in the vocabulary list at the end of the chapter. In this imitated pronunciation the Italian sounds are represented by English syllables; read each syllable as if it were part of an English word. After the third chapter we will continue to put an acute accent on those words which are not stressed on the penultimate syllable. If in doubt about pronunciation, go back to this introduction or listen carefully to the CDs.

When reading the imitated pronunciation, remember that:

ah   sounds like a in 'fast' but is shorter than in English;

oh   sounds like the o in 'order' and even the 'au' in 'caught';

eh   sounds like the e in 'poem' or even the 'ay' in 'say' but much shorter;

n'y   sounds like 'ni' in 'onion';

l'y   sounds like 'lli' in 'million';

hr   sounds something like a Scottish r.

All new words appear in the vocabulary list at the end of each chapter. If you feel doubtful about the pronunciation check the imitated pronunciation in the lists for the first three chapters.

STRESS

In Italian all words end in a vowel and are generally stressed on the next to last syllable:

albergo [ahl-<u>bair</u>-goh] hotel
finito [fee-<u>nee</u>-toh] finished
idea [ee-<u>deh</u>-ah] idea

If the stress falls on the last vowel, that vowel will have a grave accent:

caffè [kahf-fèh] coffee
perchè [paihr-kày] why

Sì ('yes') has an accent because it might otherwise be confused with **si** ('oneself'), and **è** ('is') is accented to distinguish it from **e** ('and').

If the stress falls on the last syllable but two (and rarely on the last but three), then we will put an acute accent on the stressed vowel throughout the book (although this accent is not normally shown in modern Italian):

tímido [tée-mee-doh] shy
bellíssimo [behl-lées-see-moh] very beautiful

The combinations **-ia, -io, -ie** at the end of a word are normally considered as a single syllable, so the stress falls on the preceding syllable:

Venezia [veh-neh-tsiah] Venice
doppio [dohp-pioh] double

Exceptions are marked with the acute accent:
scrivanía [skree-vah-nee-ah] desk

PRONUNCIATION OF VOWELS

The Italian vowels are **a, e, i, o** and **u**. Each vowel has only one sound, but **o** and **e** can be open or closed according to their position, as you will see below.

a	is pronounced like a in 'car' but it is shorter in Italian	**sala** [sah-lah] hall
		la [lah] the

e	is pronounced like 'ai' in said or like e in 'poem'	**letto** [leht-toh] bed **mela** [meh-lah] apple
i	is pronounced like 'ee' in 'meet'	**vino** [vee-noh] wine
o	is pronounced like o in 'not' or like o in 'almost'	**posta** [pos-tah] post **sono** [soh-noh] I am
u	is pronounced like 'oo' in 'moon'	**cura** [koo-rah] cure

PRONUNCIATION OF CONSONANTS

Most consonants are pronounced like their English counterparts. The exceptions are:

c	is pronounced like 'ch' in 'much' before **e** and **i**	**ci** [chee] there
	but it is pronounced like k in 'king' before **o, a** and **u**	**casa** [kah-zah] house
ch	is always pronounced like k in 'king'	**che** [keh] that
g	is pronounced like j in 'jeep' before **e** and **i**, but it is pronounced like g in 'go' before **a, o** and **u**	**giro** [jee-hroh] trip **gara** [gah-rah] race **guida** [gwee-dah] guide
gh	is always pronounced like g in 'gate'	**laghi** [lah-gee] lakes
gli	is pronounced like 'll' in 'million'	**luglio** [loo-l'yoh] July **gli** [l'yee] the
gn	is almost like 'ni' in 'companion'	**ogni** [oh-n'yee] every **gnocchi** [n'yohk-kee] dumplings

h	is not pronounced at all	**ha** [ah] he has
qu	is pronounced like 'qu' in 'queen'	**qui** [qwee] here **questo** [qwehs-toh] this
r	is rolled, something like a Scottish r	**caro** [kah-hroh] dear
s	is sharp as in 'see' before consonants, when double, or at the beginning of words	**strada** [strah-dah] road **sesso** [sehs-soh] sex **sala** [sah-lah] hall
	but it is like *z* in 'lazy' between two vowels	**casa** [kah-zah] home
sc	is pronounced like 'sh' in 'she' before **i** and **e**	**sci** [shee] ski **scena** [sheh-nah] scene
	but it is pronounced 'sk' as in 'skip' when followed by a consonant or by **o**, **a**, **u**	**scusa** [skoo-zah] sorry **scrivo** [skree-voh] I write
z	is pronounced like 'ts' in 'gutsy'	**pranzo** [prahn-tsoh] lunch
	or softer like 'dz' at the beginning of words	**zero** [dzeh-hroh] zero

Double consonants are emphasized and pronounced as if there were a short pause in front of them:
ditta [deet-tah] firm, *but* **dita** [dee-tah] fingers
sonno [son-noh] sleep, *but* **sono** [soh-noh] I am

On the whole, when speaking Italian you should linger on the vowels and not pronounce the consonants too forcefully (except in the case of double consonants). Remember at the end of a sentence to make your voice rise when it is a question and fall when it is a statement.

Week 1

You will learn:
- how to book a room in a hotel in Italian
- to introduce yourself, say where you come from
- to say hello and goodbye
- to use the formal form of address

The grammar includes:
- gender of nouns and adjectives
- articles 'the' (il, lo, la, l') and 'a' (un, uno, una, un')
- negative sentences
- questions
- present tense of 'to be' ('éssere') and 'to have' ('avere')
- present tense of regular '-are' verbs ('parlare')

CONVERSATION A

All'albergo   TRACK 3

Dialogue between the hotel receptionist and Mrs Branson, who is booking a room.

MRS BRANSON	**Buongiorno.**
RECEPTIONIST	**Buongiorno, signora.**
MRS BRANSON	**Ha una cámera líbera?**
RECEPTIONIST	**Sì, certo, doppia o síngola?**
MRS BRANSON	**Síngola.**
RECEPTIONIST	**Per quanti giorni?**
MRS BRANSON	**Solo per oggi.**
RECEPTIONIST	**E il Suo nome, per favore?**
MRS BRANSON	**Sono Mary Branson.**
RECEPTIONIST	**È inglese?**
MRS BRANSON	**No, sono americana.**
RECEPTIONIST	**Ha un documento, per favore?**
MRS BRANSON	**Sì, ecco il passaporto.**
RECEPTIONIST	**Beníssimo grazie, ecco la chiave.**

TRANSLATION A

At the hotel

MRS BRANSON   Good morning.
RECEPTIONIST   Good morning, madam.
MRS BRANSON   Do you have a room [free]?
RECEPTIONIST   Yes, certainly, double or single?
MRS BRANSON   Single.
RECEPTIONIST   For how long [lit. how many days]?
MRS BRANSON   Only for today.
RECEPTIONIST   And your name please?
MRS BRANSON   I'm Mary Branson.
RECEPTIONIST   Are you English?
MRS BRANSON   No, I'm American.
RECEPTIONIST   Do you have any identification [lit. document], please?
MRS BRANSON   Yes, here is my [lit. the] passport.
RECEPTIONIST   Fine, thank you, here is the key.

1 GENDER

All nouns (words which name things) in Italian are either masculine or feminine. As you have seen in the dialogue: **una cámera** is feminine (f), but **il passaporto** is masculine (m). As a general rule all nouns ending in **-a** are feminine, all nouns ending in **-o** are masculine. There are exceptions, but we will mention these later on in the book.

Nouns ending in **-e** may be either masculine or feminine. It is therefore important to remember which article is used in front of a word:

il passaporto
la cámera
la chiave
il signore

If there is an adjective (descriptive word) this too will change according to the gender of the word to which it refers:

la signora americana
But
il passaporto americano

IMITATED PRONUNCIATION (1)

eel pahs-sah-pohr-toh; lah káh-meh-hrah;
lah kiah-veh; eel see-n'yoh-hreh;
lah see-n'yoh-hrah ah-meh-hree-kah-nah;
eel pahs-sah-pohr-toh ah-meh-hree-kah-noh.

2 ARTICLES: A, AN, THE

'A' and 'an' are translated in Italian by **un** before a masculine word and **una** before a feminine one.

Una takes an apostrophe, **un'**, before a feminine word beginning with a vowel and **un** becomes **uno** before words beginning with z or with s followed by another consonant:

una cámera
un' americana
un albergo
uno studente

'The' is translated by **il** before masculine words beginning with consonants, and **lo** before masculine words beginning with **z** or with **s** followed by another consonant. **La** is used before feminine words.

L' is used before both masculine and feminine words beginning with a vowel:

il nome
lo zero
l' albergo

la chiave
l' occupazione

IMITATED PRONUNCIATION (2)

oon; oo-nah; oon; oo-noh; oo-nah káh-meh-hrah;
oon ah-meh-hree-kah-nah; oon ahl-behr-goh;
oo-noh stoo-dehn-teh; eel; loh; lah; eel noh-meh;
loh dzeh-hroh; lahl-behr-goh; lah kiah-veh;
lok-koo-pah-tzioh-neh.

3 QUESTIONS

When you want to ask a question in Italian you simply
make your voice rise at the end of the sentence. The
word order does not change.

Il Suo nome è inglese?
Is your name English?
Il Suo nome è inglese.
Your name is English.

Exercise 1

Answer the questions on conversation A using:
Sì, è ... (Yes, he/she/it is ...) *or:*
No, è ... (No, he/she/it is ...)
Example:
Question: La segretaria è inglese? (Is the hotel
receptionist English?)
Answer: No, è italiana. (No, she is Italian.)

1 Mary Branson è americana? Sì, è ...
2 L'albergo è inglese? No, è ...
3 La cámera è líbera?
4 Il passaporto è americano?
5 La camera è solo per oggi?
6 La segretaria è italiana?
7 La signora è inglese?
8 L'albergo è italiano?
9 La cámera è síngola?
10 La cámera è doppia?

IMITATED PRONUNCIATION (3)

eel soo-oh noh-meh eh in-gleh-zeh; see; noh;
seh-greh-tah-hriah; ee-tah-liah-nah; lée-beh-hrah;
sín-goh-lah; dohp-piah.

4 | NEGATIVE SENTENCES

In Italian you make a sentence negative by putting **non**
in front of the verb:

La signora non è inglese.
The lady is not English.
Mary non parla italiano.
Mary does not speak Italian.

Exercise 2

Make these sentences negative:

1 Sono di Verona.
2 Sandro Bianchi ha una bella casa.
3 L'albergo è pieno.
4 La signorina lavora in un albergo.
5 Parlate bene l'italiano?

Exercise 3

Put the correct form of **il**, **lo**, **l'**, **la** before the following words:

1 Questo è lo Zoo.
2 Parliamo bene il italiano.
3 il marito di Mary è inglese
4 Rita è la moglie di Sandro.
5 Ascolto l' ópera alla Scala.
6 la signora è italiana.
7 l' albergo è molto cómodo.
8 Questa è la cámera síngola.
9 Ecco la chiave.
10 Ecco il passaporto.

IMITATED PRONUNCIATION (4)

nohn; pahr-lah. soh-noh; be-ahn-kee; behl-lah; kah-zah;
pieh-noh; see-n'yoh-hree-nah; lah-voh-hrah;
pahr-lah-teh; beh-neh; ee-tah-liah-noh. qwehs-toh;
dzoh-oh; pahr-liah-moh; mah-hree-toh; moh-l'yeh;
ahs-kohl-toh; óh-peh-hrah; kóh-moh-doh;
qwes-tah; ehk-koh.

Al bar dell'albergo

Conversation between Mary Branson, her husband Peter, and Paolo and Anna Rossi, an Italian couple also staying at the hotel.

TRACK 7

MARY **Buongiorno.**
PAOLO **Buongiorno, signora.**
MARY **Mi chiamo Mary Branson.**
PAOLO **Piacere! Io sono Paolo Rossi.**
MARY **Piacere! Molto lieta!**
PAOLO **Questa è mia moglie.**
ANNA **Piacere!**
MARY **E questo è mio marito.**
PAOLO **Molto lieto! Parla italiano anche Lei?**
PETER **No.**
MARY **Purtroppo no. Siamo americani.**
PAOLO **Di dove siete?**
MARY **Siamo di Washington. E voi?**
PAOLO **Siamo di Milano.**
MARY **Ah! Milano è molto bella.**
ANNA **Sì, ma anche Washington è una città bella e famosa.**

TRANSLATION B

At the hotel bar

MARY   Good morning.
PAOLO Good morning, madam.
MARY   My name is Mary Branson.
PAOLO How do you do. I'm Paolo Rossi.
MARY   How do you do! Pleased to meet you.
PAOLO This is my wife.
ANNA   How do you do.
MARY   And this is my husband.
PAOLO Pleased to meet you. Do you speak Italian too?
PETER No.
MARY   Unfortunately not. We are American.
PAOLO Where are you from?
MARY   Washington. And you?
PAOLO We are from Milan.
MARY   Ah, Milan is very beautiful.
ANNA   Yes, but Washington too is a beautiful and
       famous city.

5 PRESENT TENSE OF 'ÉSSERE' (TO BE)

1st sing.	(io)	sono	I am
2nd	(tu)	sei	you (familiar) are
3rd	(lui, lei, Lei)	è	he, she is; you (formal) are
1st pl.	(noi)	siamo	we are
2nd	(voi)	siete	you (plural) are
3rd	(loro)	sono	they are

It is not necessary to use the subject pronouns **io**, **tu**, **Lei**, **lui**, **noi**, **voi** or **loro** except for emphasis.

IMITATED PRONUNCIATION (5)

(ee-oh) soh-noh; (too) seh-ee; (loo'ee/leh'ee) eh; (no-ee) see-ah-moh; (vo-ee) see-eh-teh; (loh-roh) soh-noh.

6 FORMS OF ADDRESS

In Italian there are two forms of address. When talking to children, friends and family the familiar form is used: **tu**. When addressing everybody else, it is polite to use the **Lei** form, which is in fact the third person singular of the verb. When addressing more than one person **voi** is used for both the formal and familiar forms:

Are you English?	**Sei inglese?**	(familiar singular)
	È inglese?	(formal)
	Siete inglesi?	(formal and familiar plural)

Note that capital letters are used for **Lei, Suo/Sua** etc when they mean 'you' and 'yours' (formal), to distinguish them from **lei, suo/sua** etc, which mean 'she' and 'his/hers'.

7 PRESENT TENSE OF AVERE ('TO HAVE')

ho	I have
hai	you have
ha	you (formal) have, he, she, it has
abbiamo	we have
avete	you (plural) have
hanno	they have

8 PRESENT TENSE OF -ARE VERBS

parlare (to speak)

parlo	I speak
parli	you speak
parla	you (formal) speak, he, she, it speaks
parliamo	we speak
parlate	you speak
párlano	they speak

1

All the regular verbs ending in -**are** are conjugated like **parlare** (e.g. **abitare**, **lavorare**, **ascoltare**).

Note that the stress moves to the ending in the 1st and 2nd persons plural [pahr-liah-moh, pahr-lah-teh] but reverts to the stem in the 3rd person plural [pahr-lah-noh].

IMITATED PRONUNCIATION (7/8)

oh; ah'ee; ah; ahb-be-ah-moh; ah-veh-teh; ahn-noh. pahr-lah-hreh; pahr-loh; pahr-lee; pahr-lah; pahr-liah-moh; pahr-lah-teh; páhr-lah-noh; ah-bee-tah-hreh; lah-voh-hrah-hreh; ahs-kohl-tah-hreh.

CONVERSATION C

In casa Brazzi   TRACK 9

Mary and John White have been invited to Sandro and Rita Brazzi's flat in Venice after meeting them at a symposium for wine exporters. They talk about what they do and where they live.

RITA	**Buonasera, signor White.**
MARY & JOHN	**Buonasera.**
RITA	**Questo è mio marito Sandro.**
SANDRO	**Piacere.**
JOHN	**Questa è mia moglie, Mary.**
SANDRO	**Molto lieto, signora.**
RITA	**Siete americani vero?**
MARY	**Sì, siamo di New York. E voi?**
RITA	**Siamo di Milano, ma abitiamo qui a Venezia da molti anni.**
SANDRO	**E a New York dove abitate?**
JOHN	**A Brooklyn.**
RITA	**Avete un appartamento o una casa?**
MARY	**Abbiamo una píccola casa con giardino.**
JOHN	**Sandro lavora a Venezia?**

RITA **Sì, ha un ristorante vicino a Piazza San Marco.**
MARY **Io sono insegnante. E Lei?**
RITA **Io sono una commessa. E Suo marito?**
MARY **Lavora in un albergo nel centro di New York City.**

TRANSLATION C

At the Brazzis'

RITA Good evening, Mr White.
MARY & JOHN Good evening.
RITA This is my husband Sandro.
SANDRO How do you do.
JOHN This is my wife Mary.
SANDRO Very pleased to meet you.
RITA You are American, aren't you?
MARY Yes, we are from New York. And you?
RITA We are from Milan, but we have lived in Venice for many years.
SANDRO And where do you live in New York?
JOHN In Brooklyn.
RITA Do you have a flat or a house?
MARY We have a small house with a garden.
JOHN Does Sandro work in Venice?
RITA Yes, he has a restaurant near Piazza San Marco.
MARY I am a teacher. And you?
RITA I am a shop assistant. And your husband?
MARY He works in a hotel in the centre of New York City.

Exercise 4

Read Conversation C, then answer the following questions:

1 Il signor White è inglese?
2 Come si chiama sua moglie?
3 Dove ábita Sandro?
4 Di dove sono Sandro e sua moglie?
5 Chi lavora a Venezia?
6 Il signor White lavora?
7 La moglie di Sandro è una commessa?
8 Il signor White lavora a Brooklyn?
9 Chi è insegnante?
10 Mary e John ábitano in una casa con giardino?

Exercise 5

Translate:

1 I live in Milan.
2 Do you (formal) work in Venice?
3 Where do you (formal) live?
4 I am a shop assistant.
5 Rita Rossi speaks Italian.
6 We live in Pavía and work in Milan.
7 New York City is beautiful.
8 Do you (plural) have an (use 'the') American passport?
9 Where do you (plural) come from?
10 I am American.

KEY PHRASES & VOCABULARY

Try to memorize these phrases to help you recall the main grammatical points and the subject matter of this chapter:

Ha una cámera líbera?
Sono di New York City.
Ábito a Brooklyn.
Lavoro in centro.
Parlo un po' l'italiano.

You should be familiar with the words listed below, as they have all appeared in this week. Nevertheless, check how well you've learnt them by covering up one column or the other and translating.

a [ah]	at, to, in
abitare [ah-bee-tah-hreh]	to live
albergo (m.) [ahl-behr-goh]	hotel
americano [ah-meh-hree-kah-noh]	American
anche [ahn-keh]	also, too
anno (m.) [ahn-noh]	year
appartamento (m.) [ahp-pahr-tah-mehn-toh]	flat
ascoltare [ahs-kohl-tah-reh]	to listen
avere [ah-veh-hreh]	to have
bello [behl-loh]	beautiful
beníssimo [beh-nées-see-moh]	very well
buonasera [bwoh-nah-seh-hrah]	good evening
buongiorno [bwohn-johr-noh]	good morning
cámera (f.) [káh-meh-hrah]	room
cameriere (m.) [kah-meh-hrieh-hreh]	waiter
casa (f.) [kah-zah]	home, house
centro (m.) [chen-troh]	centre
certo [chehr-toh]	sure, certainly
chi [kee]	who
chiave (f.) [kiah-veh]	key
cognome (m.) [koh-n'yoh-meh]	surname
come [koh-meh]	how
commessa (f.) [kohm-mehs-sah]	shop assistant

1

cómodo [kóh-moh-doh]	comfortable
da molti anni [dah mohl-tee ahn-nee]	for many years
di [dee]	of
di dove [dee doh-veh]	where from
documento (m.) [doh-koo-mehn-toh]	document
doppio [dohp-pioh]	double
dove [doh-veh]	where
e [eh]	and
ecco [ehk-koh]	here is, here it is
éssere [ehs-seh-hreh]	to be
famoso [fah-moh-zoh]	famous
giorno (m.) [johr-noh]	day
grazie [grah-tzieh]	thank you
il (m.) [eel]	the
inglese (m. & f.) [in-gleh-zeh]	English
insegnante (m. & f.) [in-seh-n'yan-teh]	teacher
italiano [ee-tah-liah-noh]	Italian
la (f.) [lah]	the
lavorare [lah-voh-hrah-hreh]	to work
Lei [lay]	you (sing. formal)
lei (f)	she
líbero [lée-beh-hroh]	free
lo [loh]	the
marito [mah-hree-toh]	husband
mi chiamo [mee kiah-moh]	my name is
Milano (f.) [mee-lah-noh]	Milan
mio [mee-oh]	my, mine
moglie (f.) [moh-l'yeh]	wife
molto [mohl-toh]	very, much
molto lieto [mohl-toh lieh-toh]	pleased (to meet you)
no [noh]	no
nome (m.) [noh-meh]	name
non [nohn]	not
occupazione (f.) [ok-koo-pah-tzioh-neh]	job, occupation
oggi [od-jee]	today
ópera (f.) [óh-peh-hrah]	opera
parlare [pahr-lah-hreh]	to speak

passaporto (m.) [pahs-sah-pohr-toh]	passport
Pavía (f.) [pah-vee-ah]	Pavia
per [pehr]	for
per favore [pehr fah-voh-hreh], **per piacere** [pehr piah-cheh-hreh]	please
piacere [piah-cheh-hreh]	how do you do
píccolo [pík-koh-loh]	small
pieno [pieh-noh]	full
purtroppo [poohr-trop-poh]	unfortunately
quanto [qwahn-toh]	how, how much
questo [qwehs-toh]	this
qui [qwee]	here
ristorante (m.) [hrees-toh-hran-teh]	restaurant
segretaria (f.) [seh-greh-tah-hriah]	secretary, receptionist
sì [see]	yes
si chiama [see kiah-mah]	he/she is called
signora (f.) [see-n'yoh-hrah]	Mrs, madam
signore (m.) [see-n'yoh-hreh]	Mr, sir
signorina (f.) [see-n'yoh-hree-nah]	Miss, young lady
síngolo [sín-goh-loh]	single
solo [soh-loh]	only
specialmente [speh-chahl-mehn-teh]	specially
studente (m.) [stoo-dehn-teh]	student
Suo, Sua [soo-oh, soo-ah]	your, yours
un, uno, una [oon, oo-noh, oo-nah]	a, an
un po' [oon poh]	a little
Venezia (f.) [veh-neh-tsiah]	Venice
vero [veh-hroh]	true
vicino [vee-chee-noh]	near
zero (m.) [dzeh-hroh]	zero, nought
zoo (m.) [dzoh-oh]	zoo

Week 2

You will learn to:
- talk about your home, daily routine, family and the rooms in a house
- rent a flat

The grammar includes:
- plurals of articles, nouns and adjectives
- present tense of '-ere' and '-ire' verbs: 'vivere' ('to live') and 'dormire' ('to sleep')
- possessive adjectives and pronouns: 'mio', 'tuo' etc ('my', 'mine', 'yours')
- 'C'è' ('there is') and 'ci sono' ('there are')
- prepositions: 'a', 'da', 'di', 'in', 'su'
- possession
- question words: 'che?' ('what?'), 'di chi?' ('whose?'), 'dove?' ('where?')

CONVERSATION A

In una famiglia italiana

A conversation between the Italian host, signora Silvestri, and her guest, an English student, Peter Taylor.

SILVESTRI **Buongiorno signor Taylor, e benvenuto a casa nostra.**

TAYLOR **Buongiorno signora Silvestri, piacere di conóscerla. È questa la mia cámera?**

SILVESTRI **Sì. È un po' píccola ma ha tutti i móbili necessari. E dalla finestra vede anche il Colosseo.**

TAYLOR **Sì, sì. Mi piace, è luminosa e ha anche una scrivanía per tutti i miei libri.**

SILVESTRI **Tutti i miei óspiti préndono la prima colazione qui. Va bene anche per Lei?**

TAYLOR **Sì, beníssimo. E, scusi, dov'è il bagno per favore?**

SILVESTRI **È in fondo al corridoio a destra.**

TAYLOR **Dove metto la mia valigia?**

SILVESTRI **Nello sgabuzzino vicino alla cucina.**

TAYLOR **Grazie signora. Adesso metto via la mia roba.**

With an Italian family

SILVESTRI	Good morning Mr Taylor, and welcome to our house.
TAYLOR	Good morning Mrs Silvestri, pleased to meet you. Is this my room?
SILVESTRI	Yes, it is a little small but has all the necessary furniture. From the window you can see the Colosseum.
TAYLOR	Yes, I like it. It is bright and has even got a desk for all my books.
SILVESTRI	All my guests have their breakfast here. Is that all right with you?
TAYLOR	Yes, fine. Where is the bathroom please?
SILVESTRI	At the end of the corridor on the right.
TAYLOR	Where can I put my suitcase?
SILVESTRI	In the boxroom near the kitchen.
TAYLOR	Thank you. Now I can put my things away.

2

Exercise 6

Answer the following questions about Conversation A:

1 La cámera del signor Taylor è grande?
2 Dov'è il bagno?
3 La signora Silvestri offre la colazione ai suoi óspiti?
4 Dove mette la valigia il signor Taylor?
5 Dov'è lo sgabuzzino?

9 MR, MRS, MISS, MS

Note that **signore**, **signora**, and **signorina** take the definite article when they are followed by name or surname. Note also that **signore** becomes **signor**:

Il signor Bianchi è italiano.
Mr Bianchi is Italian.
La signorina Rossi è qui.
Miss Rossi is here.

But in direct speech these articles are not used:

Buongiorno, signora Rossi.
Good morning, Mrs Rossi.

There is no equivalent to Ms in Italian, but it has now become customary to address all women as **signora**. **Signorina** is used for very young women only.

10 PLURALS OF THE ARTICLES

The Italian definite articles **il**, **lo**, **la**, **l'**, ('the') change in the plural:

	singular	plural
masculine	**il**	**i**
	lo, l'	**gli**
feminine	**la, l'**	**le**

IMITATED PRONUNCIATION (9/10)

see-n'yohr; qwee; bwohn-johr-noh. eel, ee; loh, l'yee; lah, leh.

11 PLURALS OF NOUNS AND ADJECTIVES

When you want to make a noun plural you have to change its ending:

	singular	plural
masculine	**il libro**	**i libri**
	the book	the books
	lo studente	**gli studenti**
	the student	the students
	l'ingresso	**gli ingressi**
	the hall	the halls
feminine	**la cámera**	**le cámere**
	the room	the rooms
	l'ora	**le ore**
	the hour	the hours

This rule applies also to adjectives:

la cámera ammobiliata   **le cámere ammobiliate**
the furnished room   the furnished rooms
il signore inglese   **i signori inglesi**
the English gentleman   the English gentlemen
la signorina inglese   **le signorine inglesi**
the English young lady   the English young ladies

To help you with this rule remember:

singular	plural
-o	**-i**
-e	**-i**
-a	**-e**

Note that all masculine and feminine nouns and adjectives ending in **-e** in the singular end in **-i** in the plural. Consequently, the endings of the noun and the adjective don't always match:

la casa grande   **le case grandi**
the big house   the big houses

IMITATED PRONUNCIATION (11)

eel lee-broh, ee lee-bree;loh stoo-dehn-teh,
l'yee stoo-dehn-tee; leen-gres-soh, l'yee een-gres-see;
lah káh-meh-hrah, leh káh-meh-hreh; loh-hrah,
leh oh-hreh; lah káh-meh-hrah ahm-moh-beel-yah-tah,
leh káh meh-hreh ahm-moh-beel-yah-teh;
eel see-n'yoh-hreh in-gleh-zeh,
ee see-n'yoh-hree in-gleh-zeh;
lah see-n'yoh-hree-nah in-gleh-zeh,
leh see-nyoh-hree-neh in-gleh-zee;
lah kah-zah grahn-deh, leh kah-zeh grahn-dee.

___ Exercise 7 _____

Put the following sentences into the plural:

Example:

Questo è il nostro libro. *Plural*: Questi sono i nostri libri.
Io guardo il giornale. *Plural*: Noi guardiamo i giornali.

1 Questa è la mia cámera.

2 Il bagno è occupato.

3 Io lavoro per la mia compagnía.

4 Lo studente americano studia molto.

5 La sua valigia è vuota.

6 Il pasto comincia dopo le nove.

7 Il nostro pensionante parla bene la lingua.

8 La signora arriva con la figlia.

9 Se la porta è aperta io entro.

10 L'appartamento al primo piano è spazioso.

IMITATED PRONUNCIATION

All new words in this exercise should be found in the
vocabulary list at the end of the chapter; check there for
the imitated pronunciation, should you be in any doubt.
The same applies to other exercises.

María has just moved into her new flat and describes it
to her friend Luigi.

2

LUIGI **Allora, sei contenta della tua nuova casa?**

MARÍA **Sì, abbastanza. Non è molto grande, ma almeno ci sono due cámere da letto per i bambini.**

LUIGI **Quante stanze avete in tutto?**

MARÍA **Tre cámere da letto, la sala, il tinello, la cucina e il bagno.**

LUIGI **E avete anche un bel terrazzo, vero?**

MARÍA **Sì, siamo al quarto piano con un grande terrazzo sul davanti e una sala abbastanza spaziosa.**

LUIGI **Che bello! Così potete mangiár fuori d'estate.**

MARÍA **Appunto. E desideriamo invitare tutti i nostri amici il próssimo weekend. Venite anche voi, vero?**

LUIGI **Certo, molto volentieri. Scrivi qui il tuo nuovo indirizzo. Vivete lontano dal centro?**

MARÍA **Sì, viviamo in perifería, ma c'è la metropolitana vicino.**

LUIGI **Beníssimo. Allora a sábato, ciao.**

MARÍA **Ciao Luigi. Arrivederci.**

TRANSLATION B

LUIGI	Are you happy in your new home, then?
MARÍA	Yes, quite. It is not very big but at least there are two bedrooms for the children.
LUIGI	How many rooms do you have altogether?
MARÍA	Three bedrooms, dining room, breakfast room, kitchen and bathroom.
LUIGI	And you have a beautiful terrace, don't you?
MARÍA	Yes, we are on the fourth floor with a large terrace at the front and a fairly big dining room.
LUIGI	How lovely! So you can eat outside in the summer.
MARÍA	Exactly. And next weekend we want to invite all our friends. You will come, won't you?
LUIGI	Yes, we will be pleased to. Write your new address here. Do you live far from the centre?
MARÍA	Yes, we live in the suburbs but there is the underground nearby.
LUIGI	Good. See you Saturday then. Goodbye.
MARÍA	Bye Luigi. See you soon.

Exercise 8

Answer the following questions about Conversation B:

1 Quante cámere da letto ha l'appartamento di María?
2 A che piano è?
3 Che cosa fa Luigi il próssimo weekend?
4 María vive vicino al centro?
5 C'è la metropolitana vicino alla casa di María?

Exercise 9

You live in a small house on the outskirts of London, with two bedrooms, a large kitchen and a big garden. Describe this to your business acquaintance signor Bianchi (B), who is planning to come and visit you.

Fill the gaps with the correct form of the words given in brackets:

B   Lei ábita a Londra, vero?

YOU   Sì, ma non in centro … *(I live in the suburbs)*.

B   Ah, è difficile venire a casa Sua?

YOU   No, … *(there is the underground nearby)*.

B   E una casa o un appartamento?

YOU   È … *(a small house with a large garden)*.

B   In Inghilterra ci sono molte di queste case?

YOU   Sì, al pianterreno c'è … *(a large kitchen)*.

B   E al primo piano che cosa c'è?

YOU   Ci sono … *(two bedrooms and a bathroom)*.

B   Ma la vostra casa non è troppo lontana dall'ufficio?

YOU   No, … *(it is quite near)*.

B   Siete proprio fortunati!

12 PRESENT TENSE OF '-ERE' AND '-IRE' VERBS

Italian verbs ending in **-ere** and **-ire** in the infinitive have very similar endings in the present:

	vívere (to live)	**dormire** (to sleep)
io	vivo	dormo
tu	vivi	dormi
Lei, lei, lui	vive	dorme
noi	viviamo	dormiamo
voi	vivete	dormite
loro	vívono	dórmono

Other Italian verbs like **vívere** are: **préndere** (to take),
vedere (to see), **scrívere** (to write). Verbs ending in **-ire**
and conjugated like dormire are: **sentire** (to hear),
vestire (to dress), **aprire** (to open).

There are many irregular verbs ending in **-ere** and **-ire**
and they will be explained as they occur in the book.

IMITATED PRONUNCIATION (12)

vée-veh-hreh; vee-voh; vee-vee; vee-veh;
vee-vee-ah-mo; vee-veh-teh; vée-voh-moh.
dohr-mee-reh; dohr-moh; dohr-mee; dohr-meh;
dohr-mee-ah-moh, dohr-mee-teh; dóhr-moh-noh.
préhn-deh-hreh; skree-veh-hreh; sehn-tee-hreh;
vehs-tee-hreh; ah-pree-hreh.

Exercise 10

Complete the following sentences using the correct
present tense of the verb given in brackets:

1 La signora Bianchi (vívere) in perifería.
2 I bambini (dormire) in una píccola cámera da letto.
3 Noi (préndere) il treno.
4 Voi (sentire) molto rumore dalla strada?
5 E tu perchè non (aprire) la finestra?
6 Voi (vedere) molti film alla televisione?
7 Gianni e María (vestire) con molta eleganza.
8 Voi non (sentire) mai il campanello.
9 Dove (méttere) le valigie lo studente?
10 Noi (conóscere) Firenze molto bene.

13 MY, MINE, YOUR, YOURS, ETC

In order to establish ownership you use these possessive adjectives and pronouns:

	m. sing.	f. sing.	m. pl.	f. pl.
my, mine	**mio**	**mia**	**miei**	**mie**
your, yours (*fam.*)	**tuo**	**tua**	**tuoi**	**tue**
his, her, hers	**suo**	**sua**	**suoi**	**sue**
your, yours (*form.*)	**Suo**	**Sua**	**Suoi**	**Sue**
our, ours	**nostro**	**nostra**	**nostri**	**nostre**
your, yours (*pl.*)	**vostro**	**vostra**	**vostri**	**vostre**
their, theirs	**il loro**	**la loro**	**i loro**	**le loro**

NOTE: all these adjectives and pronouns agree with the gender and number of the thing possessed, not with the possessor:

la sua casa   his house
i miei libri   my books

Note also that in Italian they are preceded by an article:

la nostra cámera   our room
i vostri pensionanti your lodgers

BUT the article is omitted with most of them before members of the family in the singular:

mio marito   my husband
sua moglie   his wife

Loro, however, is always used with an article:

il loro padre   their father

IMITATED PRONUNCIATION (13)

mee-oh, mee-ah, mee-eh'ee, mee-eh; too-oh, too-ah,
too-oh'ee, too-eh; soo-oh, soo-ah, soo-oh'ee, soo-eh;
nohs-troh, nohs-trah; nohs-tree, nohs-treh; vohs-troh,
vohs-trah, vohs-tree, vohs-treh; eel lohr-hroh,
lah lohr-hroh, ee lohr-hroh, leh lohr-hroh.

Exercise 11

Complete the following sentences using the correct
form of the possessive adjectives with or without the
articles, as in the rule in Section 13.

Example:
Questa è (my) cámera. Questa è la mia cámera.
Questa è (my) moglie. Questa è mia moglie.

1 Oggi invitiamo Mario e (his) figli.

2 (her) appartamento è al terzo piano.

3 I Bianchi vivono con (their) famiglia.

4 Vivete ancora con (your) genitori?

5 Ho un appuntamento con (my) amici.

6 Vivi con (your) madre?

7 Signora, Lei conosce (our) ditta?

8 Questo è (my) padre.

9 Signor Bianchi, dove sono (your) valigie?

10 Signori, sono queste (your) valigie?

CONVERSATION C

Un appartamento da affittare

Mrs Smith needs to rent a flat in Naples. She has found one and wants to find out from the landlord, signor Piani, as much as possible about location, facilities etc.

PIANI   **Abbiamo un appartamento ammobiliato líbero in luglio.**

SMITH   **Dov'è l'appartamento?**

PIANI   **È vicino al centro di Nápoli.**

SMITH   **C'è una scuola vicino? Perchè i miei figli vanno ancora a scuola.**

PIANI   **Sì, ci sono le scuole elementari e anche una scuola media.**

SMITH   **C'è un garage per la nostra mácchina?**

PIANI   **Sì, ma l'affitto del garage è extra.**

SMITH   **Capisco. E quante stanze ci sono?**

PIANI   **Tre cámere da letto, la sala da pranzo, il tinello, una cucina moderna e due bagni.**

SMITH   **A che piano è?**

PIANI   **Al sesto piano, ma c'è l'ascensore.**

SMITH   **L'appartamento è ammobiliato, vero? C'è tutto il necessario?**

PIANI   **Sì, c'è la lavatrice, l'aspirapólvere, la lavapiatti e forniamo anche la bianchería se desídera.**

SMITH   **Beníssimo. Abbiamo noi la bianchería, ma i miei bambini chiédono se c'è anche la televisione.**

PIANI   **Sì, certo.**

SMITH   **Ci sono negozi lì vicino? Questo è importante per noi.**

PIANI   **Sì, c'è un supermercato nella stessa strada e anche un mercato in Piazza Indipendenza.**

SMITH   **È possíbile avere le chiavi oggi per vedere l'appartamento?**

PIANI   **Certo.**

2

A flat to let

PIANI   We have a furnished flat free in July.

SMITH   Where is the flat?

PIANI   Near the centre of Naples.

SMITH   Is there a school nearby? Because my children are still at school.

PIANI   Yes, there are primary schools and a middle school.

SMITH   Is there a garage for our car?

PIANI   Yes, but the rent for the garage is extra.

SMITH   I understand. How many rooms are there?

PIANI   Three bedrooms, dining room, breakfast room, a modern kitchen and two bathrooms.

SMITH   On what floor is it?

PIANI   On the sixth, but there is a lift.

SMITH   The flat is furnished, isn't it? Is everything provided?

PIANI   Yes, there is a washing machine, a vacuum cleaner, a dishwasher and we provide linen if you wish.

SMITH   Good. We do have bedlinen but my children want to know if there is a television as well.

PIANI   Yes, certainly.

SMITH   Are there local shops? This is important for us.

PIANI   Yes, there is a supermarket in the same road and also a market in Piazza Indipendenza.

SMITH   Is it possible to have the keys today to see the flat?

PIANI   Certainly.

14 'C'È' (THERE IS) AND 'CI SONO' (THERE ARE)

As you have seen in the conversation, when you want
to use 'there is' or 'there are' in Italian you use **c'è** and
ci sono:

c'è un supermercato
there is a supermarket
ci sono negozi
there are shops

Note that **c'è** and **ci sono** remain the same with a
question and in the negative form:

C'è la metropolitana?	**No, non c'è.**
Is there the underground?	No, there isn't.
Ci sono negozi?	**Sì, ci sono molti negozi.**
Are there shops?	Yes, there are many shops.

IMITATED PRONUNCIATION (14)

cheh; chee soh-noh; soo-pehr-mehr-kah-toh;
neh-goh-dzee; meh-troh-poh-lee-tah-nah.

Exercise 12

Answer these questions concerning Conversation C as
explained above. You may answer yes/no etc, but give
a full reply if you can:

1 La signora Smith ha bambini?

2 L'affitto comprende il garage?

3 La signora desídera avere la bianchería?

4 Dov'è il mercato?

5 C'è tutto il necessario nell'appartamento?

The most commonly used prepositions are:

a	to, at
da	from, by
di	of
in	in, at
su	on

These prepositions are used in the same way as in English when they are followed by the indefinite article (**un**, **una**, **uno** or **un**):

di una signora   **a un figlio**
of a lady   to a son

But when they are followed by the definite article (**il**, **lo**, **la**, **l'**, **i**, **gli**, **le**) they contract and combine to form one word. These are all the possible forms of contracted prepositions:

	m. sing.			f. sing.	
a	**al**	**allo**	**all'**	**alla**	**all**
da	**dal**	**dallo**	**dall'**	**dalla**	**dall'**
di	**del**	**dello**	**dell'**	**della**	**dell'**
in	**nel**	**nello**	**nell'**	**nella**	**nell'**
su	**sul**	**sullo**	**sull'**	**sulla**	**sull'**

	m. pl.		f. pl.	
a	**'ai**	**agli**	**alle**	
da	**dai**	**dagli**	**dalle**	
di	**dei**	**degli**	**delle**	
in	**nei**	**negli**	**nelle**	
su	**sui**	**sugli**	**sulle**	

These are the only prepositions that have a contracted form in modern Italian. All the other prepositions which you will see in the book are separate from the following article:

per la ragazza   for the girl
con i miei figli   with my children

2

16 POSSESSION

In Italian there is no equivalent of the English 'apostrophe s' (as in 'the student's room'); possession has to be expressed by **di**, **del**, etc:

the student's room   **la stanza dello studente**

These prepositions are also used in expressions like:

the kitchen door   **la porta della cucina**

17 QUESTION WORDS: WHOSE?, WHAT?, WHERE?

When asking the question 'whose?' in Italian you say **di chi?**:

Di chi è questa casa?
Whose house is this?

'What?' is translated by **che?** or **che cosa?** (often shortened to **cosa?**):

Che/Che cosa/Cosa desídera?
What do you want?

'Where' is translated by **dove**:

Dove ábita?
Where do you live?

Exercise 13

Answer the following questions using the correct form of the contracted prepositions del, dello, dell', della, dei, degli, delle:

Example:
Di chi è questa stanza? (ragazza) È della ragazza.
Whose room is this? It is the girl's.

1 Di chi è l'appartamento?
(signor Rossi)

2 Di chi è la scrivanía ?
(studenti)

3 Di chi è questo libro?
(mio amico)

4 Di chi è la mácchina?
(signora Rossi)

5 Di chi è la cámera?
(bambini)

Exercise 14

Put the correct form of the contracted prepositions al, allo, all', alla, ai, agli, alle in the spaces provided:

Example:
La stazione è vicino … parco. La stazione è vicino al parco.

1 Il ristorante è vicino … zoo.

2 Il bar è vicino … ristorante.

3 La sala è vicino … cucina.

4 Il parco è vicino … giardini.

5 La porta è vicino … finestre.

6 I ragazzi sono vicino … albergo.

7 I libri sono vicino … studenti.

Exercise 15

Put the following sentences into the plural:

1 Trovo l'appartamento ammobiliato sul giornale.
2 La figlia della signora vive con il suo ragazzo.
3 Non vedo la differenza tra questa casa e l'altra.
4 La chiave della porta è dalla portinaia.
5 L'inquilino prende la cartolina dalla cassetta delle léttere.

Exercise 16

Put the following sentences into the singular:

1 Mettiamo la nostra mácchina in garage.
2 Partiamo per l'ufficio da soli.
3 Scrivete a vostra sorella oggi?
4 I suoi fratelli vívono qui?
5 Séntono molti rumori nelle strade affollate.

Exercise 17

Translate the following sentences:

1 Mary lives with her father in Rome.
2 My flat is near the centre of Milan.
3 Whose bedroom is this? It is the children's.
4 Their kitchen is small.
5 Where do you (plural) live, in a flat or (in) a house?

KEY PHRASES & VOCABULARY

Try to memorize these phrases to help you recall the main grammatical points and the subject matter of this chapter:

Dov'è il suo appartamento?
Quante stanze ci sono?
Di chi è questo?
Mio marito e i miei figli vívono in Italia.

You should be familiar with the words listed below, as they have all appeared in this lesson. Nevertheless, check how well you've learnt them by covering up one column or the other and translating.

abbastanza [ahb-bas-tahn-tsah]	quite, enough
affitto (m.) [ahf-feet-toh]	rent
affollato [ahf-fohl-lah-toh]	crowded
allegro [ahl-leh-groh]	cheerful
allora [ahl-loh-hrah]	then
almeno [ahl-meh-noh]	at least
amico (m.) [ah-mee-koh]	friend
amici (m. pl.) [ah-mee-chee]	friends
ammobiliato [ahm-moh-beel-yah-toh]	furnished
anche [ahn-keh]	also, too, as well
ancora [ahn-koh-hrah]	still, again, yet
aperto [ah-pehr-toh]	open
appuntamento (m.) [ahp-poon-tah-mehn-toh]	appointment
appunto [ahp-poon-toh]	precisely
aprire [ah-pree-hreh]	to open
arrivederci [ahr-ree-veh-dehr-chee]	bye-bye, goodbye
aspirapólvere (m.) [ahs-pee-hrah-póhl-veh-hreh]	vacuum cleaner
bagno (m.) [bah-n'yoh]	bathroom
bambino (m.) [bahm-bee-noh]	child
benvenuto [behn-veh-noo-toh]	welcome
bianchería (f.) [biahn-keh-hree-ah]	linen
cámera da letto (f.) [káh-meh-hrah dah leht-toh]	bedroom
cartolina (f.) [kahr-toh-lee-nah]	postcard

cassetta delle léttere (f.) [kahs-set-tah dehl-leh léht-teh-hreh]	letterbox
che, che cosa [keh koh-zah]	what
chiédere [kyéh-deh-hreh]	to ask
ciao [chaoh]	hello, goodbye
colazione (f.) [koh-lah-tzioh-neh]	breakfast
compagnía (f.) [kom-pah-n'yee-ah]	company
contento [kohn-tehn-toh]	happy
corridoio (m.) [kohr-hree-doy-oh]	corridor
così [koh-zèe]	so, like this
cucina (f.) [koo-chee-nah]	kitchen
da [dah]	from, by
davanti a [dah-vahn-tee ah]	in front of
desiderare [deh-zee-deh-hrah-hreh]	to wish
destra [dehs-trah]	right
differenza (f.) [deef-feh-hren-tsah]	difference
difficile [deef-fée-chee-leh]	difficult
ditta (f.) [deet-tah]	firm
dormire [dohr-mee-hreh]	to sleep
due [doo-eh]	two
estate (f.) [ehs-tah-teh]	summer
extra [ehks-trah]	extra
famiglia (f.) [fah-mee-l'yah]	family
figlio (m.) [fee-l'yoh]	son, child
finestra (f.) [fee-nehs-trah]	window
fratello (m.) [frah-tehl-loh]	brother
fuori [fwoh-hri]	outside
garage (m.) [gah-hrah-jeh]	garage
genitori (m. pl.) [jeh-nee-toh-hree]	parents
giardino (m.) [jahr-dee-noh]	garden
giornale (m.) [johr-nah-leh]	newspaper
grande [grahn-deh]	big
importante [im-pohr-tahn-teh]	important
indirizzo (m.) [in-dee-hreedz-zoh]	address
in fondo a [in fohn-doh ah]	at the end of
inquilino (m.) [in-qwee-lee-noh]	tenant
in tutto [in toot-toh]	altogether
invitare [in-vee-tah-hreh]	to invite
lavapiatti (f.) [lah-vah-piaht-tee]	dishwasher
lavatrice (f.) [lah-vah-tree-cheh]	washing machine
lingua (f.) [lin-gwah]	language

2

2

Londra (f.) [lohn-drah]		London
lontano da [lohn-tah-noh dah]		far from
luglio (m.) [loo-l'yoh]		July
ma [mah]		but
mácchina (f.) [máhk-kee-nah]		car
madre (f.) [mah-dreh]		mother
mangiare [mahn-jah-hreh]		to eat
Metropolitana (f.) [meh-troh-poh-lee-tah-nah]		Underground
méttere [méht-teh-hreh]		to put
móbili (m. pl.) [móh-bee-lee]		furniture
moderno [moh-dehr-noh]		modern
negozio (m.) [neh-goh-dzioh]		shop
occupato [ohk-koo-pah-toh]		busy
occupazione (f.) [ohk-koo-pah-dzioh-neh]		occupation
óspite (m. & f.) [óhs-pee-teh]		guest
padre (m.) [pah-dreh]		father
pasto (m.) [pahs-toh]		meal
pensionante (m. & f.) [pehn-sioh-nahn-teh]		paying guest
periferia (f.) [peh-hree-feh-hree-ah]		suburbs
piano (m.) [piah-noh]		floor
pianterreno (m.) [pian-tehr-hreh-noh]		ground floor
piazza (f.) [piadz-zah]		square
porta (f.) [pohr-tah]		door
portinaio (m.) [pohr-tee-nay-oh]		doorkeeper
possíbile [pohs-sée-bee-leh]		possible
potere [poh-teh-hreh]		to be able
préndere [préhn-deh-hreh]		to take, to fetch
primo [pree-moh]		first
próssimo [próhs-see-moh]		next
quarto [qwahr-toh]		fourth
ragazzo (m.) [hrah-gadz-zoh]		boy, boyfriend
roba (f.) [hroh-bah]		belongings, things
rumore (m.) [hroo-moh-hreh]		noise
sábato (m.) [sáh-bah-toh]		Saturday
sala da pranzo (f.) [sah-lah dah prahn-dzoh]		dining room

scrivanía (f.) [skree-vah-nee-ah]   desk
scrívere [skrée-veh-hreh]   to write
scuola (f.) [sqwoh-lah]   school
scuola elementare (f.)   primary school
  [eh-leh-mehn-tah-hreh]
scuola media (f.) [meh-diah]   middle school
sentire [sehn-tee-hreh]   to hear
sesto [sehs-toh]   sixth
sgabuzzino (m.)   boxroom
  [sgah-boodz-zee-noh]
sorella (f.) [soh-hrehl-lah]   sister
spazioso [spah-dzioh-zoh]   roomy
stanza (f.) [stahn-dzah]   room
su [soo]   on
supermercato (m.)   supermarket
  [soo-pehr-mehr-kah-toh]
televisione (f.)   television
  [teh-leh-vee-zioh-neh]
terrazzo (m.) [tehr-hradz-zoh]   terrace
tinello (m.) [tee-nehl-loh]   breakfast room
tra [trah]   among, between
trovare [troh-vah-hreh]   to find
valigia (f.) [vah-lee-jah]   suitcase
vedere [veh-deh-hreh]   to see
vestire [vehs-tee-hreh]   to dress
vívere [vée-veh-hreh]   to live
vuoto [vwoh-toh]   empty
weekend (m.) [week-end]   weekend
zio (m.) [dzee-oh]   uncle

2

Week 3

You will learn to:
- ask the way
- ask about tickets
- talk about public and private transport
- find out times of arrivals and departures

The grammar will include:
- demonstrative adjectives and pronouns ('this', 'that', 'those', etc)
- indefinite adjectives ('some', 'any', etc)
- numbers up to 1,000
- telling the time
- regular past participles and use of perfect tense
- irregular verbs: 'andare' ('to go') and 'fare' ('to do', 'make')

CONVERSATION A

Alla CIT

Peter Taylor wants to get to know Rome and goes to CIT (Compagnía Italiana Turismo) to ask the agency clerk, signorina Carla Sacchi, for a map of the city and information about public transport.

PETER   **Buongiorno, signorina. Scusi, ha una cartina di Roma?**

CARLA   **In inglese o in italiano?**

PETER   **In italiano, grazie. Studio l'italiano all'università e così imparo di più.**

CARLA   **Buon'idea. Éccola. Desídera qualche altra informazione? [Peter apre la cartina]**

PETER   **È questa l'università?**

CARLA   **No, quello è il politécnico. Questi sono gli istituti universitari.**

PETER   **Grazie, e c'è un áutobus o la metropolitana?**

CARLA   **Dunque, vede qui sulla carta, questa è la metropolitana, e qui c'è la fermata dell'áutobus.**

PETER **Grazie mille, signorina. Dove compro i biglietti per l'áutobus?**

CARLA **Dal tabaccaio o dal giornalaio. Ogni biglietto è válido per settantacinque minuti.**

PETER **Settantacinque minuti per qualsíasi distanza?**

CARLA **Sì, anche quando cambia áutobus.**

PETER **Grazie. Arrivederci.**

CARLA **Arrivederci e buon soggiorno.**

TRANSLATION A

At the Italian State Tourist Office

PETER Good morning, Miss. Do you have a map of Rome, please?

CARLA In English or in Italian?

PETER In Italian please. I'm studying Italian at the university and this way I learn more.

CARLA Good idea! Here it is. Do you want any other information? [Peter opens the map]

PETER Is this the university?

CARLA No, that's the polytechnic. These are the university institutes.

PETER Thank you, is there a bus or the underground?

CARLA Well, you see here on the map, this is the underground and here is the bus stop.

PETER Thank you very much. Where can I buy the tickets for the bus?

CARLA At the tobacconist's or newsagent's. Each ticket is valid for 75 minutes.

PETER 75 minutes whatever the distance?

CARLA Yes, even when you change bus.

PETER Thank you. Goodbye.

CARLA Goodbye and have a nice stay.

Exercise 18

Read or listen to Conversation A carefully, then answer the following questions:

1 Dove va Peter?
2 Che cosa desídera?
3 Dove compra i biglietti per l'áutobus?
4 Per quanti minuti è válido un biglietto?

18 THIS, THAT, THOSE, ETC

The demonstrative adjective and pronouns 'this' and 'these' are translated by:

questo (m. sing.)
questa (f. sing.)
questi (m. pl.)
queste (f. pl.)

These adjectives and pronouns are regular in all their forms:

questo áutobus è in ritardo
this bus is late
questa è la Sua cartina
this is your map
questi sono gli istituti
these are the institutes
queste fermate sono obbligatorie
these are compulsory stops

'That' and 'those' are translated by:

quel, quell', quello (m. sing.)
quella, quell' (f. sing.)
quei, quegli (m. pl.)
quelle (f. pl.)

Note that the masculine forms have the same endings as the definite articles (**il, lo, l', i, gli**) according to whether the word that follows begins with a vowel or a consonant. So you use:

quel   when you would use **il**
(before consonants)

quell'   when you would use **l'**
(before vowels)

quello   when you would use **lo**
(before **z**, **s** + consonant, **gn**)

quei   when you would use **i**
(before consonants)

quegli   when you would use **gli**
(before vowels, **z**, **s** + consonant, **gn**)

Examples:

Quel semáforo non funziona.
Those traffic lights don't work.
Quell'áutobus è in orario.
That bus is on time.
Quello studente è inglese.
That student is English.
Quella motocicletta è pericolosa.
That motorcycle is dangerous.
Quell'automóbile è guasta.
That car is not working.
Quei viaggiatori sono seduti.
Those travellers are seated.
Quegli sportelli sono aperti.
Those doors are open.
Quelle gomme sono sgonfie.
Those tyres are flat.

BUT this is only true of demonstrative adjectives. The demonstrative pronouns (i.e. when **quello**, **quelli**, **quella** and **quelle** are used on their own) have regular endings in the singular and in the plural:

Quello è l'ufficio informazioni.
That's the information office.
Quelli sono tutti posti prenotati.
Those are all booked seats.

Note that these pronouns also translate the English 'the one/the ones':

Quel posto è occupato, prendo quello vicino al finestrino.
That seat is taken, I am taking the one near the window.

IMITATED PRONUNCIATION (18)

kwehs-toh, kwehs-tah, kwehs-tee, kwehs-teh;
ów-toh-boos; hree-tahr-doh; kahr-tee-nah;
is-tee-too-tee; fehr-mah-teh; ohb-blee-gah-toh-hree-eh;
kwehll; kwehl-loh; kwehl-lah; kweh'ee; kwehl-l'yee;
kwehl-leh.
For the pronunciation of nouns in the remaining model sentences, consult the vocabulary list at the end of this chapter.

_____ Exercise 19 _____

Change the following sentences using quel, quell', quello, quella, quei, quegli, quelle instead of the definite articles.
Example:
I treni sono veloci.→ Quei treni sono veloci.

1 La cartina è gratis.
2 L'áutobus è affollato.
3 Il treno è veloce.
4 Lo scompartimento è riservato.
5 Partite con gli amici di Emma?
6 Porti le valigie in stazione?
7 I biglietti sono di andata e ritorno.
8 Gli orari non sono giusti.
9 Parti con l'aéreo?
10 Sono líberi i posti?

Exercise 20

Translate the following sentences:

1 This is my seat.
2 These tickets are valid for three hours.
3 These are my Italian guests.
4 We take that train.
5 Is that the bus stop?
6 Those children are English.
7 We travel on that bus.
8 Those are my suitcases.
9 That [train] door is open.
10 This is the station.

19 INDEFINITE ADJECTIVES (SOME, ANY, ETC)

The indefinite adjectives are **qualche** (some), **ogni** (every), **qualsíasi/qualunque** (any, whatever).

ogni vagone
every/each carriage
qualche ora
some hours
qualsíasi distanza
whatever distance
qualunque autostrada
any motorway

Note: these indefinite adjectives are ALWAYS singular in Italian:

Qualche treno arriva in orario.
Some trains arrive on time.

IMITATED PRONUNCIATION (19)

kwahl-keh; oh-n'yee; kwahl-sée-ah-see; kwahl-oon-kweh; vah-goh-neh; oh-hrah; dees-tahn-tzah; ow-toh-strah-dah; treh-noh; oh-hrah-hrioh.

CONVERSATION B

Alla fermata dell'áutobus

Peter is now at the bus stop waiting to catch the bus to the university. Signora Mazzi, who is also waiting there, starts talking to him.

SIGNORA **Prende anche Lei il trédici?**
PETER **Veramente non sono sicuro. Qual è l'áutobus per l'università?**
SIGNORA **Quello è il venticinque e passa ogni dieci minuti.**
PETER **Scusi, che ore sono adesso?**
SIGNORA **Sono le úndici e mezzo.**
PETER **Grazie, signora. E Lei dove va?**
SIGNORA **Ho un appuntamento con mia figlia, in Piazza Navona a mezzogiorno.**
PETER **Quanto ci vuole in áutobus?**
SIGNORA **Circa un quarto d'ora. Ma, vede quell'áutobus? È il venticinque. È proprio fortunato Lei!**

TRANSLATION B

At the bus stop

MRS MAZZI Are you also taking the 13?
PETER I'm not sure actually. Which is the bus for the university?
MRS MAZZI That's the 25 and there is one every 10 minutes.
PETER What's the time, please?
MRS MAZZI Half past eleven.
PETER Thank you. Where are you going?
MRS MAZZI I have an appointment with my daughter in Piazza Navona at midday.
PETER How long does it take by bus?
MRS MAZZI About a quarter of an hour. But do you see that bus? It's the 25, you are really lucky!

Exercise 21

Read or listen to Conversation B several times and, when you are sure you remember the key points, answer these questions:

1 Dove va l'áutobus 13?
2 Che ore sono?
3 A che ora ha appuntamento la signora?
4 Quanto ci vuole per andare in Piazza Navona?
5 Che áutobus va all'università?

20 NUMBERS

1	uno	16	sédici
2	due	17	diciassette
3	tre	18	diciotto
4	quattro	19	diciannove
5	cinque	20	venti
6	sei	30	trenta
7	sette	40	quaranta
8	otto	50	cinquanta
9	nove	60	sessanta
10	dieci	70	settanta
11	úndici	80	ottanta
12	dódici	90	novanta
13	trédici	100	cento
14	quattórdici	200	duecento
15	quíndici	1,000	mille

NOTE: all numbers in Italian are written as one word. So:

23	ventitrè
197	centonovantasette
865	ottocentosessantacinque

BUT: when using tens and units you drop the endings of **venti**, **trenta**, **quaranta** etc before **uno** and **otto**:

21	ventuno	31	trentuno
41	quarantuno	28	ventotto
38	trentotto	48	quarantotto

IMITATED PRONUNCIATION (20)

oo-noh; doo-eh; treh; kwaht-troh; cheen-kweh; say'ee;
seht-teh; oht-toh; noh-veh; dee-ay-chee; óon-dee-chee;
dóh-dee-chee; treh-dee-chee; kwaht-tóhr-dee-chee;
kwín-dee-chee; séh-dee-chee; dee-chahs-seht-teh;
dee-choht-toh; dee-chahn-noh-veh; vehn-tee;
trehn-tah; kwah-hrahn-tah; cheen-kwahn-tah;
sehs-sahn-tah; seht-tahn-tah; oht-tahn-tah;
noh-vahn-tah; chehn-toh; doo-eh-chehn-toh;
meel-leh. vehn-tee-tréh; chehn-toh noh-vahn-tah
seht-teh; oht-toh chehn-toh sehs-sahn-tah cheen-kweh;
vehn-too-noh; vehn-toht-toh.

21 TELLING THE TIME

To ask What's the time? in Italian you say: **Che ore
sono?** or **Che ora è?** The answer is: **Sono le ...** followed
by the hour and then the minutes.

it is 5.30	**sono le cinque e mezzo**
it is 6.00	**sono le sei**
it is 6.15	**sono le sei e un quarto**
it is 6.45	**sono le sei e tre quarti**
it is 5.45	**sono le sei meno un quarto**
it is 6.05	**sono le sei e cinque**
it is 6.55	**sono le sei e cinquantacinque**
it is 5.55	**sono le sei meno cinque**

Note that **mezzogiorno** (midday), **mezzanotte** (midnight)
and **l'una** (one o'clock) are used with **è**:

it is midday	**è mezzogiorno**
it is midnight	**è mezzanotte**
it is one o'clock	**è l'una**

Note also that instead of using 'a.m.' or 'p.m.' in Italian
you use the 24-hour system:

it is 8.20 p.m.	**sono le venti e venti**

To ask At what time …?(i.e. when something happens) you say **a che ora**:

At what time does the bus leave?
A che ora parte l'áutobus?
At 4.30.
Alle quattro e mezzo.
At one o'clock.
All'una.
At midnight.
A mezzanotte.

Exercise 22

Write down the time in Italian as in the examples below:

12.30   È mezzogiorno e mezzo.
 7.45   Sono le sette e tre quarti/Sono le otto meno un quarto.

1	2.30	**6**	4.45
2	3.00	**7**	8.35
3	21.00	**8**	1.30
4	12.15	**9**	2.50
5	24.00	**10**	7.10

Exercise 23

Change the following statements into questions and answer using 'a che ora'. For example:

Il treno parte alle 8. Question: A che ora parte il treno?
                        Answer: Alle otto.

1 L'áutobus parte alle 6.
2 L'aéreo parte alle 7.30.
3 Il treno parte alle 22.30.
4 Il treno arriva alle 17.25.
5 L'áutobus arriva alle 13.15.

CONVERSATION C

Alla stazione

Peter Taylor is at the Stazione Términi in Rome to meet his
friend Luisa, who has just arrived from Siena.

PETER **Ciao Luisa, finalmente sei arrivata!**
LUISA **Scusa, Peter, ma il treno è partito in ritardo
già da Siena.**
PETER **Non importa. Sei stanca adesso? A che ora
sei partita da casa?**
LUISA **Sono partita da casa alle sei! Prima sono
andata in bicicletta fino alla stazione e poi
ho aspettato il treno per un'ora.**
PETER **Allora, andiamo súbito a mangiare
qualcosa. Ho già prenotato il ristorante.**
LUISA **Beníssimo, grazie Peter. Hai avvisato la tua
padrona di casa?**
PETER **Certo. E ha già preparato la cámera per te.**

TRANSLATION C

At the station

PETER Hello Luisa, you've arrived at last!
LUISA Sorry, Peter, but the train was late when it left
Siena [lit. left already late from Siena].
PETER It's all right. Are you tired? What time did you
leave home?
LUISA I left at six! First I went by bike to the station
and then I waited one hour for the train.
PETER Then let's go and eat straight away. I have
already booked the restaurant.
LUISA Fine, thank you, Peter. Have you warned the
landlady?
PETER Yes. She has already got the room ready for you.

22 PAST PARTICIPLES

Preparato, **venduto**, **finito** (prepared, sold, finished) are the past participles of **preparare**, **véndere** and **finire**. They are formed by removing **-are**, **-ere**, **-ire** from the infinitive and adding **-ato**, **-uto**, **-ito**.

23 TALKING ABOUT THE PAST

3

When you want to talk about what you have done, seen etc in the past, in Italian you use the perfect tense. This is formed as follows:

1 For most verbs by using the present tense of **avere** (to have) and the past participle:

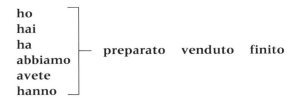

ho
hai
ha
abbiamo ── preparato   venduto   finito
avete
hanno

Examples:
Ieri Marco ha preparato il pranzo.
Yesterday Mark prepared lunch.
Ieri abbiamo venduto la casa.
Yesterday we sold the house.
Ieri ho finito alle 9.
Yesterday I finished at 9.

2 By using the present tense of **éssere** (to be) followed by the past participle with intransitive verbs (i.e. verbs which have no direct object). These include the verbs of motion: 'to go', 'to arrive', 'to leave', and of lack of motion, 'staying', like **stare***, **rimanere** etc:

*Note that **stare** and **éssere** are the same in the perfect tense: **sono stato/a** (I have been/stayed) etc.

	andare		cadere	
	to go		to fall	
sono	andato,	andata	caduto,	caduta
sei	"	"	"	"
è	"	"	"	"
siamo	andati,	andate	caduti,	cadute
siete	"	"	"	"
sono	"	"	"	"

	partire	
	to leave	
sono	partito,	partita
sei	"	"
è	"	"
siamo	partiti,	partite
siete	"	"
sono	"	"

Note that with these verbs the past participle must agree with the subject:

María è caduta. Mary (f.) has fallen/fell.
Marco è caduto. Mark (m.) has fallen/fell.
Gli studenti sono andati.
The students (m. pl.) have gone/went.
Le ragazze sono state qui.
The girls (f. pl.) have been [stayed] here.

Exercise 24

Answer the following questions on Conversation C:

1 Dove è andato Peter?
2 Perchè è arrivata in ritardo Luisa?
3 Da dove è partita Luisa?
4 Che cosa ha prenotato Peter?
5 Che cosa ha preparato la padrona di casa?

Exercise 25

Change the following sentences using 'ieri' (yesterday) and the past tense:

Example:

Luisa arriva alle tre.→ Ieri Luisa è arrivata alle tre.

1 Mario arriva alle tre.
2 Il treno parte alle nove.
3 L'áutobus arriva in ritardo.
4 María parte con il treno.
5 I signori Bianchi arrívano alle due.
6 Le valigie cádono per terra.
7 La signorina va in mácchina.
8 Noi (f.) partiamo all'una.
9 Voi (m.) andate in treno?
10 I viaggiatori vanno a préndere il taxi.

Exercise 26

Change these sentences using 'un'ora fa' (an hour ago) and the perfect tense of the verbs:

Examples:

Preparo la cámera.→ Un'ora fa ho preparato la cámera.
Sentiamo la radio.→ Un 'ora fa abbiamo sentito la radio.

1 Guido la mácchina.
2 Mangio il pranzo.
3 María prepara la colazione.
4 Vendiamo la nostra mácchina.
5 Cómprano i biglietti.
6 I passeggeri guárdano l'orario.
7 Senti questo rumore?
8 Finiamo il pranzo.
9 Prenotiamo il ristorante.
10 Pórtano le valigie sul treno.

Un viaggio d'affari

Francesca has just returned from a business trip to
Sardinia and tells her husband Marino what she has done
and seen there.

FRANCESCA	**Ciao Marino, finalmente sono arrivata.**
MARINO	**Ciao. Com'è andato il volo?**
FRANCESCA	**Bene. Ma l'aéreo ha fatto scalo ad Alghero e il volo è durato tre ore.**
MARINO	**Sei stata sempre a Cágliari?**
FRANCESCA	**No, ho preso una mácchina a noleggio e sono andata anche a Nuoro per due giorni.**
MARINO	**Ci sono stato anch'io. È bella vero?**
FRANCESCA	**Sì, molto, ma non ho avuto molto tempe per vedere la città.**
MARINO	**Hai firmato quel famoso contratto per il nuovo albergo?**
FRANCESCA	**Sì, ho deciso di accettare la loro offerta. E ho anche visto il nuovo direttore.**
MARINO	**Bene. Hai fatto molto.**
FRANCESCA	**Eh sì, ma la próssima volta vorrei restare più a lungo. E tu, cos'hai fatto di bello?**
MARINO	**Anch'io ho lavorato molto. Ma, vedi, ho anche preparato il tuo piatto preferito per stasera.**
FRANCESCA	**Fantástico! Sei stato bravo.**

A business trip

FRANCESCA	Hello Marino, I've arrived at last.
MARINO	Hello. How was the flight?
FRANCESCA	Fine, but the plane stopped in Alghero and the flight lasted three hours.
MARINO	Did you stay in Cagliari all the time?
FRANCESCA	No, I hired a car and went to Nuoro as well for two days.
MARINO	I've been there too. It's beautiful, isn't it?
FRANCESCA	Yes, very. But I didn't have much time to see the town.
MARINO	Did you sign that famous contract for the new hotel?
FRANCESCA	Yes, I decided to accept their offer. I saw the new manager too.
MARINO	Good. You've done a lot.
FRANCESCA	Yes, but next time I'd like to stay longer. And what have you been doing?
MARINO	I worked hard too. But, look, I've also prepared your favourite dish for tonight.
FRANCESCA	Great! You've been really good.

3

24 IRREGULAR VERBS

Here are five verbs whose irregularities include the past participle (and, therefore, the perfect tense):

decídere:	**deciso**	**ho deciso**	I have decided, I decided
éssere:	**stato**	**sono stato, stata**	I have been
fare:	**fatto**	**ho fatto**	I have done, I did
préndere:	**preso**	**ho preso**	I have taken, I took
vedere:	**visto**	**ho visto**	I have seen, I saw

Both the following present tenses are irregular:

fare (to do, make) **andare** (to go)
faccio **vado**
fai **vai**
fa **va**
facciamo **andiamo**
fate **andate**
fanno **vanno**

Exercise 27

You have just arrived from Sardinia and your host (O) asks you about your journey. Complete the dialogue using the clues given:

   o Buongiorno signor Taylor, ben arrivato.
      Com'è andato il viaggio?

YOU (Very well, thank you. But my plane left late from Rome. So I arrived late in Cagliari.)

   o A che ora è partito da Roma?

YOU (At 10.45, but I left home at 7 o'clock.)

   o Ha preso il taxi dall'aeroporto?

YOU (No, I hired a car.)

   o C'è sempre molto tráffico, vero?

YOU (Yes, but I decided to hire the car for one week.)

   o È un'óttima idea, così è più fácile visitare la città e i dintorni.

YOU (I have not seen the centre. I would like to go to all the famous places.)

Exercise 28

Rewrite Conversation D as a report of what Francesca did in Sardinia, beginning with Oggi Francesca è tornata …

Try to memorize these key phrases covering the grammar and topics of this week:

Quel ragazzo ha preso l'áutobus.
A che ora parte il treno?
Parte alle diciannove.
Ieri sono andata in Sardegna.

3

You should be familiar with the words listed below, as they have all appeared in this week. Nevertheless, check how well you've learnt them by covering up one column or the other and translating.

aéreo (m.) [ah-éh-hreh-oh]	aeroplane
aeroporto (m.) [ah-eh-hroh-pohr-toh]	airport
affari (m. pl.) [af-fah-hree]	business
affollato [af-fohl-lah-toh]	crowded
albergo (m.) [ahl-behr-goh]	hotel
Alghero (f.) [ahl-geh-hroh]	Alghero
andare [ahn-dah-hreh]	to go
andata e ritorno (biglietto di) [ahn-dah-tah eh hree-tohr-noh]	return (ticket)
arrivare [ahr-ree-vah-hreh]	to arrive
aspettare [ahs-peht-tah-hreh]	to wait for
áutobus (m.) [ów-toh-boos]	bus
automóbile (f.) [ow-toh-móh-bee-leh]	car
autostrada (f.) [ow-toh-strah-dah]	motorway
avvisare [ahv-vee-zah-hreh]	to warn
bicicletta (f.) [bee-chee-kleht-tah]	bicycle
biglietto (m.) [bee-l'yeht-toh]	ticket
bravo [brah-voh]	good, clever
cadere [kah-deh-hreh]	to fall
Cágliari (f.) [káh-l'yah-hree]	Cagliari
cambiare [kahm-byah-hreh]	to change
caro [kah-hroh]	dear, expensive

cartina, carta (f.) [kahr-tee-nah, kahr-tah]	map
chiesa (f.) [kieh-zah]	church
città (f.) [cheet-tàh]	town, city
ci vuole [chee-vwoh-leh]	it takes
comprare [kom-prah-hreh]	to buy
con [kon]	with
contratto (m.) [kon-traht-toh]	contract
corso (m.) [kohr-soh]	road, high street
costare [kos-tah-hreh]	to cost
decídere [deh-chée-deh-hreh]	to decide
di più [dee pyòo]	more
direttore (m.) [dee-hreht-toh-hreh]	director
diritto [dee-hreet-toh]	straight
distanza (f.) [dees-tahn-tzah]	distance
dunque [doon-qweh]	so, then
durata (f.) [doo-hrah-tah]	duration
éccola [éhk-koh-lah]	here she/it is
fácile [fáh-chee-leh]	easy, simple
fantástico [fahn-táhs-tee-koh]	fantastic
fare [fah-hreh]	to do, make
fermata (f.) [fehr-mah-tah]	stop
ferrovía (f.) [fehr-roh-vee-ah]	railway
finalmente [fee-nahl-mehn-teh]	at last
finire [fee-nee-hreh]	to finish
fino a [fee-noh ah]	until
giornalaio (m.) [johr-nah-lay-oh]	newsagent
giusto [joos-toh]	right
gomma (f.) [gohm-mah]	tyre
gratis [grah-tees]	free
guasto [gwahs-toh]	broken down, not working
guidare [gwee-dah-hreh]	to drive
idea (f.) [ee-deh-ah]	idea
imparare [im-pah-hrah-hreh]	to learn
informazione (f.) [in-fohr-mah-dzioh-neh]	information
in orario [in oh-hrah-hrioh]	on time
in ritardo [in hree-tahr-doh]	late
istituto (m.) [is-tee-too-toh]	institute, faculty
lezione (f.) [leh-dzioh-neh]	lesson

mezzanotte (f.) [mehdz-zah-noht-teh]	midnight
mezzo [mehdz-zoh]	half
mezzogiorno (m.) [mehdz-zoh-johr-noh]	midday
mille grazie [meel-leh grah-tzieh]	many thanks
minuto (m.) [mee-noo-toh]	minute
motocicletta (f.) [moh-toh-chee-kleht-tah]	motorcycle
museo (m.) [moo-zeh-oh]	museum
noleggio (m.) [noh-lehj-joh]	hire
obbligatorio [ohb-blee-gah-toh-hrioh]	compulsory
offerta (f.) [ohf-fehr-tah]	offer
ogni [oh-n'yee]	every
ora (f.) [oh-hrah]	hour
orario (m.) [oh-hrah-hrioh]	timetable
padrona (f.) [pah-droh-nah]	landlady
partire [pahr-tee-reh]	to leave
passare [pahs-sah-hreh]	to pass, spend, go by
passeggero (m.) [pahs-sehj-jeh-hroh]	passenger
per terra [pehr tehr-hrah]	on the floor
perchè [pehr-kèh]	why, because
piatto (m.) [piaht-toh]	dish, plate
più a lungo [pyóo ah loon-goh]	longer (time)
poi [poy]	then
politécnico (m.) [poh-lee-téhk-nee-koh]	polytechnic
portare [pohr-tah-hreh]	to carry
posto (m.) [pohs-toh]	seat, place
pranzo (m.) [prahn-tzoh]	lunch
preferito [preh-feh-hree-toh]	favourite
prenotare [preh-noh-tah-hreh]	to book
preparare [preh-pah-hrah-hreh]	to prepare
proprio [proh-prioh]	really, quite
qual, quale [kwahl, kwah-leh]	which
qualche [kwal-keh]	some
qualcosa [kwahl-koh-zah]	something
qualsíasi [kwahl-sée-ah-see]	whatever, any
qualunque [kwahl-oon-kweh]	whatever, any
quando [kwahn-doh]	when

3

radio (f.) [hrah-dioh]	radio
riservato [hree-zehr-vah-toh]	reserved, booked
ritardo (m.) [hree-tahr-doh]	delay
ritornare/tornare [hree-tohr-nah-hreh]	to go/come back, return
salire [sah-lee-hreh]	to climb, go up
scéndere [shéhn-deh-reh]	to go down, to descend
scompartimento (m.) [skohm-pahr-tee-mehn-toh]	compartment
seduto [seh-doo-toh]	seated
semáforo (m.) [seh-máh-foh-hroh]	traffic lights
sempre [sehm-preh]	always
sgonfio [zgohn-fioh]	flat (tyre)
sicuro [see-koo-hroh]	sure
soggiorno (m.) [sohj-johr-noh]	stay
sportello (m.) [spohr-tehl-loh]	door (of car, train)
stanco [stahn-koh]	tired
stasera [stah-seh-hrah]	tonight
studiare [stoo-diah-hreh]	to study
tabaccaio (m.) [tah-bahk-kay-oh]	tobacconist
taxi (m.) [tahk-see]	taxi
tráffico (m.) [tráhf-fee-koh]	traffic
treno (m.) [treh-noh]	train
ufficio informazioni (m.) [oof-fee-choh in-fohr-mah-dzioh-nee]	enquiry desk
università (f.) [oo-nee-vehr-see-tàh]	university
vagone (m.) [vah-goh-neh]	carriage
válido [váh-lee-doh]	valid
veloce [veh-loh-cheh]	fast
véndere [véhn-deh-hreh]	to sell
veramente [veh-hrah-mehn-teh]	really
vettura (f.) [veht-too-hrah]	carriage
via (f.) [vee-ah]	street
volo (m.) [voh-loh]	flight
volta (f.) [vohl-tah]	time
vorrei [vohr-reh-ee]	I would like

Week 4

You will learn to:
- book a room
- talk to an agent about buying property
- ask about facilities at a campsite

The grammar includes:
- modal verbs ('want', 'must', 'can')
- verbs ending in '-isco': 'finire', 'pulire', 'capire'
- the imperative
- irregular verbs: 'venire' ('to come'), 'tenere' ('to keep'), 'dare' ('to give'), 'stare' ('to stay')
- numbers from 1,000 to 1,000,000,000
- date: year, months, days of the week

CONVERSATION A

All'agenzia di soggiorno

Rita is on holiday on Lake Garda and is looking for cheap accommodation. At the local tourist agency she talks to Gianni:

GIANNI	**Buongiorno signora, desídera?**
RITA	**Vorrei restare a Garda per due settimane. Ci sono pensioni non troppo care?**
GIANNI	**La pensione completa costa novanta euro al giorno come mínimo.**
RITA	**Preferisco qualcosa di meno caro.**
GIANNI	**Può andare in campeggio: quíndici euro per notte più l'affitto della tenda.**
RITA	**Ci sono anche cámere in case private?**
GIANNI	**Certo, ma deve fissare il prezzo con la padrona. Vuole guardare la lista?**
RITA	**Grazie, volentieri. E qual è il prezzo di solito?**
GIANNI	**Dai venticinque ai trentacinque euro per notte.**
RITA	**Cosi è meglio per me. Grazie della lista. Arrivederci.**

At the tourist agency

GIANNI Good morning, may I help you?

RITA I would like to stay in Garda for two weeks. Are there any cheap boarding houses?

GIANNI Full board is 90 euro a day minimum.

RITA I'd prefer something cheaper.

GIANNI You can go to a campsite: 15 euro a day plus the hire of the tent.

RITA Are there rooms in private houses as well?

GIANNI Yes, but you must arrange the price with the landlady. Do you want to see the list?

RITA Yes, I'd be pleased to. What's the price usually?

GIANNI From 25 to 35 euro a night.

RITA That's better for me. Thank you for the list. Goodbye.

25 MODAL VERBS: WANT, CAN, MUST

In Italian, 'want' is **volere**, 'can' is **potere**, and 'must' is **dovere**. As in English, Italian modal verbs are used with the infinitive of the following verb:

vuole guardare	you (formal) want to look at
può andare	you (formal) can go
deve fissare	you (formal) must arrange

Note that these verbs are irregular in the present:

volere	**potere**	**dovere**
voglio (I want)	**posso** (I can)	**devo** (I must)
vuoi	**puoi**	**devi**
vuole	**può**	**deve**
vogliamo	**possiamo**	**dobbiamo**
volete	**potete**	**dovete**
vógliono	**póssono**	**dévono**

Note also that, as in English, when you say what you want it is more polite to say **vorrei** (I would like):

vorrei restare   I would like to stay

(For more information on this form of the verb see week 5, section 34.)

Exercise 29

Translate into Italian:

1 Rita wants to rent a flat.
2 Can't I look at this list?
3 I would like to book a room.
4 We cannot pay much.
5 We must leave at 9.
6 Do you (pl.) want to go to the camp site?
7 They can come today.
8 He must pay more.
9 Do you (formal) want to stay in a boarding house?
10 If I can I want to stay in Venice for three days.

26 VERBS ENDING IN '-ISCO'

There is a group of verbs ending in **-ire** which form the present tense by adding **-isc** in front of most of the endings:

finire (to finish)

finisco
finisci
finisce
finiamo
finite
finíscono

Other verbs like **finire** are:

preferire	**preferisco**	I prefer
pulire	**pulisco**	I clean
capire	**capisco**	I understand

Exercise 30

Answer the following questions, addressed to you in the formal form, using 'voglio', 'posso' or 'devo' plus infinitive and expression given:

Example:
Quando deve partire? ... adesso
Devo partire adesso.

Quando vuole andare? ... all'una
Voglio andare all'una.

1 Quando deve andare? ... più tardi
2 Dove deve aspettare? ... alla stazione
3 Chi deve vedere? ... la mia padrona di casa
4 Quando vuole venire? ... alle tre
5 Dove vuole restare? ... all'albergo
6 Chi vuole vedere? ... i miei amici
7 Quando può venire? ... a mezzogiorno
8 Dove può restare? ... al campeggio
9 Chi può invitare? ... una collega
10 Quando può pagare? ... stasera

CONVERSATION B

All'agenzia immobiliare

Hugh O'Sullivan wants to buy a small house in Umbria and is looking at various properties with signora Dossi, the estate agent:

DOSSI **Ho preparato una lista di varie proprietà come vuole Lei.**

HUGH **Guardi, io non posso spéndere più di settantacinquemila dollari.**

DOSSI **Cioè più o meno settantacinquemila euro. Per quel prezzo abbiamo appartamenti non restaurati a Gubbio e anche qualche casetta fuori.**

HUGH **Vorrei una casetta in campagna, ma le case quanto cóstano?**

DOSSI **Ci sono rústici per ottantamila euro, ma dévono éssere rimodernati.**

HUGH **Capisco, ma ci sono l'acqua e la luce eléttrica?**

DOSSI **Sì. Prenda questi fogli con le fotografie e tutti i particolari delle case. Controlli dove sono sulla piantina e vada pure a vedere dal di fuori.**

HUGH **Óttima idea. E se voglio visitare l'interno, teléfono.**

DOSSI **Ma se vuole vedere diverse case, teléfoni al mattino, così ho più tempo.**

TRANSLATION B

At the estate agency

DOSSI I have prepared a list of various properties as you wanted.

HUGH But you see, I cannot spend more than 75,000 dollars.

DOSSI That is more or less 75,000 euro. For that price we have unrestored flats in Gubbio and also some small houses outside.

HUGH I'd like a small country house, but how much are they?

DOSSI There are farmhouses for 80,000 euro but they need modernizing.

HUGH I see, but is there water and electric light?

DOSSI Yes. Take these papers with photos and all the details of the houses. Check where they are on the map and do go and see them from the outside.

HUGH Very good idea. And if I want to see the inside I will phone.

DOSSI But if you want to see several houses, phone in the morning when I have more time.

Exercise 31

Read the dialogue carefully, then answer the following questions:

1 Che tipo di proprietà vuole il signor O'Sullivan?
2 Dove preferisce abitare?
3 Può trovare un appartamento a Gubbio per settantacinquemila euro?
4 Il signor O'Sullivan può visitare l'interno delle case?
5 C'è l'acqua in questi rústici?

27 IMPERATIVE

When you want to ask or tell people to do something for you, you use the imperative. These are the familiar, formal and plural forms of the imperative:

parlare	préndere	sentire	finire
(tu) parla!	prendi!	senti!	finisci!
(Lei) parli!	prenda!	senta!	finisca!
(noi) parliamo!	prendiamo!	sentiamo!	finiamo!
(voi) parlate!	prendete!	sentite!	finite!

Examples:
Carlo, parla piano!
Speak slowly, Charles. (fam.)
Signora Rossi, prenda questo posto!
Take this seat, Mrs Rossi. (form.)
Ragazzi, finite il cómpito!
Finish your homework, boys.
Entrate, signori!
Come in, gentlemen!
Parliamo italiano!
Let's talk Italian.

NOTE: If you want to ask a favour you use **un po'** or **per favore** and if you want to encourage or allow someone to do something you use **pure** after the imperative.

Posso fumare? Certo, fumi pure!
May I smoke? Yes, please do!
Ragazzi, venite un po' qui!
Do come here, boys.

But it is quite polite to use the imperative even without any of these expressions in Italian. In particular the polite way of attracting someone's attention is to use **senta** (literally it means 'hear!'):

to a stranger: **Senta, signora, sa dov'è la stazione?**
to a friend/child: **Senti, cosa fai oggi?**

Exercise 32

Reply using the formal form of the imperative.
Example:
Scusi, devo provare?→ Sì, provi pure!

1 Scusi, devo scrívere?
2 Scusi, devo cominciare?
3 Scusi, devo finire?
4 Scusi, devo mangiare?
5 Scusi, devo pulire?
6 Scusi, devo chiúdere?
7 Scusi, devo servire?
8 Scusi, devo guardare?
9 Scusi, devo partire?
10 Scusi, devo entrare?

Exercise 33

Reply as in Exercise 32, but use the familiar form of
the imperative.
Example:
Scusa, devo provare?→ Sì, prova pure!

Exercise 34

Change the questions and answers in Exercise 32 into
the plural.
Example:
Scusate, dobbiamo provare?→ Sì, provate pure!

28 NEGATIVE IMPERATIVE

If you want to tell people what not to do you put **non** in front of the imperative in the formal or plural forms:

non entri!
non entrate!
non entriamo!

BUT in the familiar form you use **non** and the infinitive:

Carlo, entra!   *but*   **Carlo, non entrare!**

Exercise 35

Change all these sentences into the negative.
Example:
María, apri la porta!→ María, non aprire la porta!
Signora, apra la porta!→ Signora, non apra la porta!

1 Signorina, chiuda la finestra per favore!
2 Mario, porta la mia valigia per favore!
3 Piero, guarda la televisione per favore!
4 Signorina, prenda la chiave per favore!
5 María, prendi la chiave per favore!
6 Ragazzi, guardate questo salotto per favore!
7 Ragazze, prendete questa strada per favore!
8 Signor Rossi, guardi là per favore!
9 Scendiamo insieme le scale!
10 Sandro, prendi l'ombrello!

29 IRREGULAR PRESENTS

venire	tenere	dare	stare
to come	to keep	to give	to stay
vengo	**tengo**	**do**	**sto**
vieni	**tieni**	**dai**	**stai**
viene	**tiene**	**dà**	**sta**
veniamo	**teniamo**	**diamo**	**stiamo**
venite	**tenete**	**date**	**state**
véngono	**téngono**	**danno**	**stanno**

Note that **stare** is used in many idiomatic expressions in Italian which in English would require a variety of other verbs.

Examples:
Come sta?
How are you?
stare tranquillo/calmo/ fermo
to keep quiet/calm/still
stare bene/male
to feel well/unwell
stare attento
to pay attention

30 IRREGULAR IMPERATIVES

Note that the **Lei** form of the imperative is obtained from the stem of the first person singular of the present (this applies to both regular and irregular verbs):

	present	imperative
parlare	**parlo**	**parli**
sentire	**sento**	**senta**
venire	**vengo**	**venga**
tenere	**tengo**	**tenga**
andare	**vado**	**vada**
fare	**faccio**	**faccia**

BUT the following verbs have irregular imperatives:

	éssere	avere	dare	stare
(tu)	sii	abbi	da'	sta'
(Lei)	sia	abbia	dia	stia
(noi)	siamo	abbiamo	diamo	stiamo
(voi)	siate	abbiate	date	state

Examples:
Sta' fermo!
Keep still!
Sia paziente!
Be patient!
Stia calma!
Keep calm!
Non abbia paura!
Don't be afraid!
Dia una bella mancia!
Give a good tip!
Siate gentili!
Be kind!

4

Exercise 36

Answer the following questions using the formal form as in the example:

Question: Vengo anch'io?
Answer: Sì, certo, venga pure.

1 Vado anch'io?
2 Sto qui anch'io?
3 Faccio io?
4 Do anch'io i soldi?
5 Tengo il resto?
6 Vengo anch'io?
7 Finisco io?
8 Pulisco anche la cucina?
9 Bevo anch'io il vino?
10 Leggo anch'io la lista?

THE EURO

The euro is always singular and its approximate value is 60 pence. It is divided into 100 centesimi.

Example:
Questa rivista costa due euro e dieci (centesimi).
This magazine costs € 2.10.

MORE NUMBERS

In Italian a written number has a full point separating every thousand or multiple of thousand:

1.000	**mille**
1.350	**milletrecentocinquanta**
2.000	**duemila**
3.000	**tremila**
100.000	**centomila**
1.000.000	**un milione**
1.000.000.000	**un miliardo/un bilione**

Note: **mille** becomes **-mila** in the plural.

32 DAYS OF THE WEEK, MONTHS AND DATES

Giorni della settimana	Days of the week
lunedì	Monday
martedì	Tuesday
mercoledì	Wednesday
giovedì	Thursday
venerdì	Friday
sábato	Saturday
doménica	Sunday

Mesi	Months
gennáio	January
febbráio	February
marzo	March
aprile	April
maggio	May
giugno	June
luglio	July
agosto	August
settembre	September
ottobre	October
novembre	November
dicembre	December

Note that days and months are written without a capital letter.

DATES

When saying the date in Italian you use cardinal numbers (i.e. 'two', 'three', 'four' etc not 'second', 'third', 'fourth') followed by the month and the year.

The year is read like any other number. A number such as 1500 will be read as 'one thousand five hundred' and not as 'fifteen hundred'.

2 December 2001   **2 dicembre 2001**
                      (il due dicembre duemilauno)

BUT you use **primo** (first), for the first day of the month:

1st July 2002   **1 luglio 2002**
                     (il primo luglio duemiladue)

When mentioning the year you use **nel**:

in 1900   **nel 1900 (nel millenovecento)**

Exercise 37

Answer the following questions as in the example:
Example:
Che giorno è oggi? ... Wednesday.→ Oggi è mercoledì.

1	Che giorno è oggi?	... Tuesday
2	Qual è la data?	... 31st January 2002
3	Quanto costa la Sua casa?	... €100.000
4	Quanto costa il rústico?	... €85.000
5	Quanto cóstano le cartoline?	... €0.30
6	Quanti abitanti ha Verona?	... 300.000
7	Quando è finita la guerra?	... in 1945
8	Quando è nata (was born) Sofia Loren?	... in 1932
9	Quanto costa il biglietto?	... €6.65
10	Quanto costa l'aéreo per Milano?	... €120

CONVERSATION C

Al campeggio

Tony and his friend have arrived at the Campeggio Miramare and talk to the owner, signora Calvi:

TONY **Senta signora, c'è posto per la nostra roulotte qui?**

CALVI **Avete prenotato?**

TONY **No, mi dispiace.**

CALVI **Beh, vediamo. Per quanti giorni e per quante persone?**

TONY **Siamo in due, e vorremmo restare almeno una settimana.**

CALVI **Per una settimana, fino al 6 agosto, va bene.**

TONY **Possiamo vedere prima il posto?**

CALVI   **Certo. Andiamo! Vedete, queste sono le docce, qui c'è la cucina e la lavandería e questi sono i gabinetti.**

TONY   **Scusi, non capisco, che cos'è la lavandería?**

CALVI   **È il posto dove può lavare la Sua roba.**

TONY   **Ah, ho capito! E dove possiamo fare la spesa?**

CALVI   **Qui al campeggio c'è un supermercato e a Garda ci sono tutti i negozi.**

TONY   **Beníssimo. Allora lo prendiamo.**

TRANSLATION C

At the campsite

TONY   Excuse me, is there room for our caravan here?

CALVI   Have you booked?

TONY   No, sorry.

CALVI   Well, it depends. How many days and for how many people?

TONY   It's two of us and we'd like to stay at least a week.

CALVI   For one week, until August 6, it is all right.

TONY   Can we see the pitch first?

CALVI   Certainly. Let's go. These are the showers, here is the kitchen and the launderette, and these are the toilets.

TONY   Excuse me, but what is the 'launderette'?

CALVI   It is the place where you can do your washing.

TONY   I see. Where can we do the shopping?

CALVI   There is a supermarket here on the site and in Garda there are all the shops.

TONY   Excellent. We'll take it.

Exercise 38

Read Conversation C carefully, checking all new expressions, then try to answer these questions without looking at the text:

1 Che servizi ci sono al campeggio?
2 Tony e il suo amico hanno la tenda?
3 Hanno prenotato il posto prima?
4 Póssono fare la spesa al campeggio?

Exercise 39

Translate the following sentences:

1 They must book the room before August.
2 They didn't go to (in) Italy in 1989.
3 We prefer a flat on the ground floor.
4 They want to buy a house in the country.
5 Can we look at the farmhouse next week?
6 The appointment is for next Friday at 3 p.m.
7 The estate agent can arrange a visit in the morning.
8 I would like to come but today I must stay at home.
9 I am sorry but I want a room with bathroom.
10 Don't buy (formal) this house, it is too far from the centre.

Vorrei venire ma non posso.
Signora, guardi un po' questo appartamento!
Il 6 agosto tutti dévono partire.
Tenga pure il resto!

As you can see, we have now dispensed with the 'imitated pronunciation'; you ought to know the rules by now, but if in doubt consult a good dictionary or listen to the CDs.

4

acqua (f.)	water
affittare	to rent
affitto (m.)	rent
anno (m.)	year
avere paura	to be afraid
balcone (m.)	balcony
campeggio (m.)	camp site
capire	to understand
caro	dear, expensive
casetta (f.)	small house, cottage
centesimo (m.)	cent
chiúdere	to close
cioè	that is (i.e.)
cómpito (m.)	homework
dare	to give
data (f.)	date
di fuori/fuori	outside
diverso	different
diversi (pl.)	several
doccia (f.)	shower
dovere	to have to, must
fissare	to arrange
foglio (m.)	sheet of paper
fumare	to smoke
gabinetto (m.)	lavatory, toilet
guardare	to look at
interno (m.)	inside
lavandería (f.)	wash house, launderette
lista (f.)	list
luce (f.)	light

mancia (f.)	tip
mattino (m.)	morning
meno	less
mi dispiace	I am sorry
mínimo (m.)	minimum
nato	born
notte (f.)	night
oggi	today
paziente	patient
pensione completa (f.)	full board
piano	slowly
piantina (f.)	map
preferire	to prefer
prezzo (m.)	price
pulire	to clean
restaurare	to restore
rimodernare	to modernize
roulotte (f.)	caravan
rústico (m.)	farmhouse
salotto (m.)	lounge, drawing room
scale (f. pl.)	stairs
scéndere	to go down
servire	to serve
servizi (m. pl.)	facilities
settimana (f.)	week
spesa (f.)	shopping
stare	to stay, to be
stare attento	to pay attention, to be careful
stare calmo	to keep calm
tardi	late
tassa di soggiorno (f.)	tourist tax
tenda (f.)	tent
tenere	to keep
troppo	too, too much
venire	to come
volentieri	willingly
volere	to want, wish
vorremmo	we would like

4

Week 5

You will learn:
- how to order a drink and a meal
- to accept or refuse offers of drink and food
- to invite others for drinks and meals

The grammar will include:
- personal object pronouns ('me', 'you', 'us', etc)
- conditional ('I should/would...')
- imperatives with pronouns
- irregular verbs: 'bere', 'cuócere', 'dire', 'sapere'
- difference between two verbs for 'can': 'sapere' and 'potere'
- likes and dislikes: 'mi piace/non mi piace'
- uses of the preposition 'da'

CONVERSATION A

Al bar dell'albergo

Bill White is having a drink at the bar with Nina Fazzini, another guest at the hotel.

BILL	**Che cosa prende da bere?**
NINA	**Io prenderei un aperitivo analcólico, e Lei?**
BILL	**Io prendo un Martini.**
NINA	**Se permette, oggi offro io.**
BILL	**Ma no, mi ha già invitato ieri.**
NINA	**Si figuri. Il Martini, lo preferisce secco o rosso?**
BILL	**Rosso, grazie.**
NINA	**Éccoli. Salute!**
BILL	**Salute! Allora Le posso offrire una tartina?**
NINA	**Grazie, la prendo proprio volentieri.**
BILL	**Sì, le fanno buone, qui.**
NINA	**È la loro specialità.**
BILL	**Ne prendiamo un'altra?**
NINA	**Sì grazie. E un altro aperitivo?**

TRANSLATION A

At the hotel bar

BILL   What would you like to drink?
NINA   I'll have a non-alcoholic aperitif, and you?
BILL   I'll have a Martini.
NINA   Allow me, today it's my turn.
BILL   Thank you, but you treated me yesterday.
NINA   Don't mention it. Do you prefer your Martini dry or sweet?
BILL   Sweet, please.
NINA   Here they are. Cheers!
BILL   Cheers! May I offer you a canapé?
NINA   Thank you, I'd love to try one.
BILL   Yes, they make good canapés here.
NINA   It is their speciality.
BILL   Shall we have another?
NINA   Yes, please. And another aperitif?

Exercise 40

Read Conversation A carefully, then answer these questions using 'lo', 'la' or 'le' followed by the verb.
Example:
La signora Fazzini prende un Martini?→ No, non lo prende.

1   Il signor White prende un aperitivo analcólico?
2   Chi offre l'aperitivo?
3   Chi offre la tartina?
4   Il signor White prende un Martini?
5   Nina e Bill mángiano le tartine?

Object pronouns, both direct (me, him, etc) and indirect (to me, to him, etc), are used more often in Italian than in English, so it is important for you to learn to recognize them. It is also necessary to try to use them yourself.

Take, for example, the question 'Do you know this lady?' In English you'd reply 'Yes, I do' or 'No, I don't.' But the modal verb 'do' does not exist in Italian, so the polite way to answer would be to repeat the verb, in which case you must also use the pronoun:

Conosce la signora?   **No, non la conosco.**
                            Sì, la conosco.

These pronouns in Italian go before the verb, except with an infinitive and some forms of the imperative as you will see later on in this week's lesson.

And in case you think that using personal object pronouns (like the one above) may sound impolite, please remember that this is not the case in Italian; in fact quite the opposite.

direct pronouns   indirect pronouns

me	**mi**	**mi**	to me
you (fam.)	**ti**	**ti**	to you (fam.)
him, it (m.)	**lo**	**gli**	to him
her, it (f.)	**la**	**le**	to her
you (form.)	**La***	**Le***	to you (form.)
us	**ci**	**ci**	to us
you (pl.)	**vi**	**vi**	to you (pl.)
them (m.)	**li**	**gli/(loro)****	to them
them (f)	**le**		

* As with **Lei, Suo, Sua** etc, it is customary to use a capital letter for **La** and **Le** in the formal form.

** Note that the indirect pronoun **gli** has now taken the place of **loro** in everyday speech.

Note that **mi** and **ti**, **ci** and **vi** are used as both direct and indirect object pronouns:

he sees me	**mi vede**
and	
he speaks to me	**mi parla**
he sees you (pl.)	**vi vede**
and	
he speaks to you (pl.)	**vi parla**

BUT in the third person you have different pronouns:

he sees him	**lo vede**
but	
he speaks to him	**gli parla**
he sees her	**la vede**
but	
he speaks to her	**le parla**
he sees you	**La vede**
but	
he speaks to you	**Le parla**
he sees them (m.)	**li vede**
he sees them (f.)	**le vede**
but	
he speaks to them (m. & f.)	**gli parla (parla loro)**

Exercise 41

Answer these questions using the direct object pronouns 'lo', 'la', 'li', 'le':

Examples:
Prende spesso l'aperitivo?→ Sì, lo prendo spesso.
Beve spesso la birra?→ Sì, la bevo spesso.

1 Guarda spesso la televisione?
2 Compra spesso le patate?
3 Invita spesso i Suoi amici?
4 Beve spesso il caffè?
5 Prende spesso il treno?
6 Porta spesso la cravatta?
7 Mangia spesso le tartine?
8 Beve spesso vini francesi?
9 Non beve vini italiani?
10 Invita spesso la Sua vicina?

Exercise 42

Answer these questions using the indirect object pronouns 'gli', 'le':

Examples:
Quando parla a María?→ Le parlo adesso.
Quando parla a Giovanni?→ Gli parlo adesso.

1 Quando parla a Sua moglie?
2 Quando parla al direttore?
3 Quando teléfona a Giuseppe?
4 Quando risponde a Laura?
5 Quando scrive agli studenti?
6 Quando scrive alle ragazze?
7 Quando risponde a Giuseppe e María?
8 Quando teléfona al padrone di casa?
9 Quando parla ai signori Bianchi?
10 Quando scrive alla signora Rossi?

Exercise 43

Replace the words in bold with suitable direct or indirect object pronouns:

Example:
Il padre guarda **la televisione**.→ Il padre *la* guarda.
Non parlo **a Giovanni**.→ Non *gli* parlo.

1 Anna dà il número **a María**.
2 Non sento **il rumore**.
3 Il signor Forti legge **la lista**.
4 La signora prende **le olive**.
5 Compriamo **i biglietti** qui.
6 Offro l'aperitivo **ai signori Danzi**.
7 Teléfono **al mio ragazzo**.
8 Scrivete **a vostra madre**?
9 Che cosa portate **a vostro fratello**?
10 Il signor Rossi non lascia **la mancia**.

5

CONVERSATION B

In ostería

Tony and his friend Jeff have been invited by some Italian people to join them at their local bar. Tony talks to María, one member of the group.

MARÍA **Allora Tony cosa prendi?**

TONY **Io vorrei un espresso e Jeff dice che lascia fare a te.**

MARÍA **Guarda che questa è un'osteria, dove si beve soprattutto vino. Non è un posto per turisti!**

TONY **Beníssimo, allora un bicchiere di bianco per Jeff e un caffè per me, se fanno il caffè.**

MARÍA **Sì, sì il caffè c'è, ma perchè non lo prendi anche tu corretto, come me?**

TONY	**Perchè no, ma perméttimi di pagare, oggi.**
MARÍA	**Ma no, figúrati!**
TONY	**No, no, insisto, oggi tocca a me!**
MARÍA	**Come vuoi, e grazie. Salute!**
TONY	**Salute!**

TRANSLATION B

At the bar

MARÍA	What will you have, Tony?
TONY	I'd like an espresso coffee and Jeff says that it's up to you.
MARÍA	This is [like] a bar, mind you, where people drink mainly wine. It is not a tourist place.
TONY	Fine, a glass of white wine for Jeff and a coffee for me, if they do coffee.
MARÍA	Yes, there is coffee, but why don't you have it with a shot of spirits like me?
TONY	Why not, but allow me to pay today.
MARÍA	No, no, I wouldn't hear of it.
TONY	No, I insist, today it is my turn.
MARÍA	As you wish, thank you. Cheers!
TONY	Cheers!

5

____Exercise 44 ____

Read the conversation carefully, checking all new expressions, then answer these questions:

1 Che cosa beve María?

2 Tony beve il vino?

3 Che cos'è un'ostería?

4 Chi offre da bere oggi?

5 Chi beve vino bianco?

34 CONDITIONAL: ('I WOULD DO...')

In Italian, as in English, the conditional is used when we want to say what we would do. It is formed by adding the following endings to the infinitive:

-i
-sti
-bbe
-mmo
-ste
-bbero

Note that **-are** verbs change the **-a** into **-e**:

parlare	préndere	dormire
parlerei	prenderei	dormirei
parleresti	prenderesti	dormiresti
parlerebbe	prenderebbe	dormirebbe
parleremmo	prenderemmo	dormiremmo
parlereste	prendereste	dormireste
parlerébbero	prenderébbero	dormirébbero

Note also that the endings of the conditional are always regular, but the stem of some irregular verbs contracts:

avere:	avrei
éssere:	sarei
vedere:	vedrei
venire:	verrei
volere:	vorrei
dovere:	dovrei
potere:	potrei
bere:	berrei
tenere:	terrei
andare:	andrei

Examples:
Verrei volentieri.
I would come with pleasure.
Potrébbero stare qui.
They could stay here.
Andresti da solo?
Would you go alone?

Exercise 45

Answer the following questions addressed to you, changing the present tense to the conditional and using the expression given.

Examples:
Volete andare in treno?→ Sì, ... ma costa troppo.
Sì, vorremmo andare ma costa troppo.
Vuole andare in treno?→ Sì, ... ma costa troppo.
Sì, vorrei andare ma costa troppo.

1 Dovete partire oggi?   Sì, ... ma abbiamo cambiato idea.
2 Deve andare a vedere la casa?   Sì, ... ma non ho la mácchina.
3 Può venire oggi?   Si, ... ma più tardi.
4 Potete accompagnarlo?   Sì, ... in mácchina.
5 Vuole telefonare?   Sì, ... ma non ho la moneta.
6 Volete viaggiare in aéreo?   Sì, ... ma non da soli.
7 Vuole un aperitivo?   No, ... un cappuccino.
8 Volete mangiare adesso?   No, ... alle due.
9 Può venire in mácchina?   No, ... in bicicletta.
10 Dovete restare in albergo?   Sì, ... per la cena.

35 IMPERATIVE WITH OBJECT PRONOUNS

Direct and indirect object pronouns always come after the imperative, infinitive and **ecco** and are attached to them as one word. The stress does not alter. The infinitive loses its final **e**:

permettétemi!
allow me! (pl.)
préndilo!
take it! (fam.)
non prénderlo
don't take it! (fam.)
potete accompagnarlo?
can you accompany him?
éccoli
here they are
dimmi la verità
tell me the truth (fam.)

Note that in the formal form of the imperative the object pronouns go before the verb:

mi scusi!
excuse me! (form.)
non lo prenda!
don't take it! (form.)

This is because the **Lei** form of the imperative is in fact borrowed from the present subjunctive. And with this, as with all other finite tenses, the object pronouns go before the verb.

Note also that when **da'**, **di'**, **fa'**, **sta'** are followed by object pronouns these pronouns take a double consonant: **dammi** (give me), **dillo** (say it), **falle** (do them) etc.

Exercise 46

Answer the questions with the formal form of the imperative and the appropriate object pronoun 'lo', 'la', 'li', 'le', 'gli':

Example:
Che ne pensa, compro la casa?→ Sì, la compri!

1 Che ne pensa, compro il rústico?
2 Che ne pensa, mangio la minestra?
3 Che ne pensa, parlo alla signorina?
4 Che ne pensa, vendo gli appartamenti?
5 Che ne pensa, prenoto le cámere?
6 Che ne pensa, faccio la fotografia?
7 Che ne pensa, do la mancia?
8 Che ne pensa, porto i bambini?
9 Che ne pensa, teléfono al signor Bianchi?
10 Che ne pensa, prendo l'arrosto?

5

Exercise 47

Reply as in Exercise 46, but this time imagine that the conversation takes place between two friends. Use the familiar form of the imperative and practise saying 'yes' and 'no'.

Example:
Che ne pensi, compro la casa?→ Sì, cómprala!
                                 No, non comprarla!

36 IRREGULAR VERBS: 'BERE', 'DIRE', 'SAPERE'

Notice how irregular these three verbs are in the present tense:

bere (to drink)   **dire** (to say)   **sapere** (to know)

bevo	**dico**	**so**
bevi	**dici**	**sai**
beve	**dice**	**sa**
beviamo	**diciamo**	**sappiamo**
bevete	**dite**	**sapete**
bévono	**dícono**	**sanno**

37 IRREGULAR PAST PARTICIPLES: 'BERE', 'CUÓCERE', 'DIRE'

	past participle	
bere	**bevuto**	drunk
cuócere	**cotto**	cooked
dire	**detto**	said, told

38 TWO WORDS FOR 'CAN': 'SAPERE', 'POTERE'

Sapere means you have acquired a certain skill or knowledge:

So nuotare.
I can swim (I know how to swim).
So parlare italiano.
I can speak Italian (I have learnt to speak it).
Non so léggere.
I cannot read (I never learnt to read).
But:
Non posso nuotare se il mare è mosso.
I cannot swim if the sea is rough.
Non posso léggere se non ho gli occhiali.
I cannot read if I don't have my glasses.

5

Exercise 48

Fill the spaces with the correct form of 'sapere' or 'potere' in the present tense.

Example:

Non abbiamo la mácchina e non … venire.

Non abbiamo la mácchina e non possiamo venire.

1 È troppo stanco, non … giocare a tennis.

2 Studio l'italiano e lo … capire abbastanza bene.

3 Prendi lezioni di piano e non … suonare?

4 Vorrei andare al nuovo ristorante ma non … dov'è.

5 Il bar è chiuso, [noi] non … préndere la bíbita.

6 Mio marito … cucinare bene.

7 Pierino è piccolo e non … ancora scrívere.

8 Scusi, [io] … usare il teléfono?

9 Oggi i ragazzi non … nuotare.

10 È pericoloso andare in mácchina con Mario: non … guidare.

39 LIKES AND DISLIKES: 'MI PIACE / NON MI PIACE'

To say that you like something in Italian you use the verb **piacere**. This verb has a different construction from the English. Perhaps it might help you learn it if you remember that literally **mi piace** means 'it is pleasing to me'. It is always used with an indirect object pronoun:

mi
ti
gli
Le ─ **piace/piácciono**
ci
vi
gli

You use **piace** when it is followed by an infinitive or by a word in the singular:

Le piace l'italiano?
Do you (form.) like Italian?
Le piace nuotare?
Do you (form.) like swimming?
[lit. Does swimming please you?]

and **piácciono** when the following word is plural:

Mi piácciono gli spaghetti al dente!
I like spaghetti slightly undercooked.

Exercise 49

Answer the following questions using 'mi piace' or 'mi piácciono'. Example:

Le piace quella casa?→ Sì, mi piace moltíssimo.

Le piácciono quegli appartamenti?→ Sì, mi piácciono moltíssimo.

1 Le piace quel ristorante?
2 Le piácciono le lasagne al forno?
3 Le piace viaggiare?
4 Le piace il vitello?
5 Le piácciono gli zucchini?

and now answer saying what you don't like.

Example:
Le piace questa casa?→ No, non mi piace.
Le piácciono quei rústici?→ No, non mi piácciono.

6 Le piácciono i rumori?
7 Le piace fare niente?
8 Le piácciono le zanzare?
9 Le piace aspettare?
10 Le piácciono le persone noiose?

Da Mamma Rosa

Luigi has invited three of his English friends out for a meal at Mamma Rosa's, a small trattoría located in the Trastevere district of Rome, to celebrate his birthday. He is met there by the owner.

ROSA **Buongiorno, signore. Ha prenotato?**

LUIGI **Sì, ho prenotato per quattro.**

ROSA **Prego, accomodátevi qui. Le dico cosa abbiamo oggi, così potete decídere. Volete cominciare tutti con l'antipasto o no?**

LUIGI **Sì, un bell'antipasto misto per tre, ma il mio amico è vegetariano, cosa ci sarebbe per lui?**

ROSA **Abbiamo insalata russa e mozzarella con pomodoro. Va bene?**

LUIGI **Beníssimo. E per primo?**

ROSA **Ci sono ravioli di ricotta e spinaci, spaghetti all' Amatriciana e gnocchi alla Romana.**

LUIGI **Gnocchi per due, un piatto di spaghetti per me e i ravioli per la signora, per favore.**

ROSA **E per secondo? Abbiamo trota alla griglia, braciole di maiale e cotolette alla milanese.**

LUIGI **Prendiamo tutti e tre le cotolette, ma è possíbile avere un piatto di verdura per il mio amico?**

ROSA **Certo, posso portargli i finocchi al forno, e una bella scelta di altre verdure fresche. E voi cosa prendete di contorno?**

LUIGI **Per noi insalata mista e patate fritte.**

ROSA **E da bere?**

LUIGI **Acqua minerale frizzante e una caraffa di vino rosso della casa.**

5

At Mamma Rosa's

ROSA   Good morning, sir. Have you booked?

LUIGI   Yes, I booked for four.

ROSA   Please take a seat here. I'll tell you what we have today and then you can decide. Do you all want to start with hors d'oeuvre?

LUIGI   Yes we do, a mixed hors d'oeuvre for three, but my friend is vegetarian, what could he have?

ROSA   We have Russian salad and mozzarella with tomatoes. Is that all right?

LUIGI   Fine. And for the first course?

ROSA   There are ravioli with ricotta and spinach, spaghetti with Amatriciana sauce and gnocchi.

LUIGI   Gnocchi for two, spaghetti for me and ravioli for the lady.

ROSA   And for the main course? We have grilled trout, pork chops and veal cutlets.

LUIGI   We'll have cutlets for three, but is it possible to have a vegetable dish for my friend?

ROSA   Certainly, I can give him baked fennel and a choice of other fresh vegetables. And what will you have as vegetables?

LUIGI   Mixed salad and chips for us.

ROSA   And to drink?

LUIGI   Sparkling mineral water and a carafe of red house wine.

Exercise 50

Read Conversation C very carefully, then try to answer these questions using object pronouns where possible:

1 Chi vorrebbe solo un piatto di verdura per secondo? E perchè?
2 Che cosa c'è di contorno da Mamma Rosa oggi?
3 Préndono tutti i ravioli per primo?
4 Luigi órdina il vino bianco?
5 C'è solo carne per secondo?
6 Quante persone mángiano l'insalata?

40 USES OF THE PREPOSITION 'DA'

When you want to talk about going to or staying at somebody's house, office, etc in Italian you use **da** followed by the person's name or occupation:

Oggi vado dal dentista.
Today I am going to the dentist.
Ieri sono stata da María.
Yesterday I stayed at Maria's.
Compro la verdura dal fruttivéndolo.
I buy vegetables at the greengrocer's.

Da is also used (like 'for' in English) to describe a continuous period of time.

Examples:
Da quanto tempo ábita a Londra?
How long have you lived in London?
Abito a Londra da tre anni.
I have lived in London for three years.
Studio l'italiano da due mesi.
I have been studying Italian for two months.

Note that in these expressions in Italian you must use the present tense, whereas in English the perfect tense is used.

Exercise 51

Translate the following sentences:

1 We don't like to travel by train.
2 Do you (form.) like chips?
3 Please give (form.) this key to signora Rossi.
4 Would you (fam.) go by yourself?
5 Mary, don't take (fam.) my car, take yours.
6 We have given him all the necessary information.
7 Can I offer you (pl.) something to drink?
8 How long have you (pl.) been studying Italian?
9 They would buy the flat, but it costs €100,000.
10 We went to Tony's for lunch.

5

Le posso offrire qualcosa?
Mi porti un antipasto misto.
María, pórtagli gli spaghetti!
Non so nuotare.
Mi piacerebbe avere una casa in Italia.

accomodátevi	make yourselves comfortable, sit down
acqua minerale (f.)	mineral water
aglio (m.)	garlic
agnello (m.)	lamb
al dente	slightly undercooked (pasta or rice)
al forno	baked
analcólico	non-alcoholic
antipasto (m.)	hors d'oeuvre
antipasto misto (m.)	hors d'oeuvre of cooked meat (salami, ham, etc)
aperitivo (m.)	aperitif
arrosto (m.)	roast
bere	to drink
bianco	white
bíbita (f.)	soft drink
bicchiere (m.)	glass
bistecca (f.)	steak
braciola (f.)	chop
caffè (m.)	coffee
caffè corretto (m.)	coffee with a dash of spirits
caraffa (f.)	carafe
carne (f.)	meat
cena (f.)	dinner, supper
cenare	to dine
chiuso	closed
contorno (m.)	side dish
cotoletta (f.)	veal cutlet
cotoletta alla milanese	veal cutlet coated in breadcrumbs
cuócere	to cook
cotto	cooked
cravatta (f.)	tie
cucinare	to cook

5

da solo	alone
dentista (m.& f.)	dentist
dire	to say
espresso (m.)	espresso coffee
figúrati (fam.)	you are welcome
(si figuri form.)	
finocchio (m.)	fennel
forno (m.)	oven
fresco	fresh
frizzante	fizzy, sparkling
fruttivéndolo (m.)	greengrocer
giocare	to play (a game)
gnocchi (m. pl.)	potato dumplings
gnocchi alla	semolina dumplings, baked in
romana (m. pl.)	the oven
griglia (f.)	grill
insalata (f.)	salad
insístere	to insist
lasagne (f. pl.)	lasagne
lasciare	to leave
maiale (m.)	pig, pork
mancia (f.)	tip
manzo (m.)	beef
mare (m.)	sea
minerale	mineral
minestra (f.)	soup
mi piace/piácciono	I like
moneta (f.)	loose change, coins
mosso	rough (sea)
noioso	boring
nuotare	to swim
occhiali (m. pl.)	spectacles
oliva (f.)	olive
ostería (f.)	pub
patata (f.)	potato
patate fritte (f. pl.)	chips
perméttere	to allow
pesce (m.)	fish
piano, pianoforte (m.)	piano
pisello (m.)	pea
pomodoro (m.)	tomato

pranzo (m.)	lunch
primo (piatto) (m.)	first course
ravioli (m. pl.)	ravioli
ricotta (f.)	type of cream cheese
rispóndere	to reply
rosso	red
russo	Russian
salute!	cheers!
sapere	to know how
scelta (f.)	choice
se	if
secco	dry
secondo (piatto) (m.)	main (second) course
soprattutto	mainly
spaghetti (m. pl.)	spaghetti
specialità (f.)	speciality
suonare	to play (an instrument)
tartina (f.)	canapé, small snack
telefonare	to phone
tocca a me	it is my turn
trota (f.)	trout
vegetariano	vegetarian
verdura (f.)	vegetable(s)
viaggiare	to travel
vitello (m.)	veal
zanzara (f.)	mosquito
zucchino (m.)	courgette

5

Week 6

You will learn to:
- buy food, clothes and presents
- go to the bank
- ask for your size in clothes and shoes
- complain about and return purchases

The grammar will include:
- the direct object pronoun 'ne'
- agreement of perfect tense with pronouns
- double pronouns ('he gives it to me')
- ordinal numbers (first, second, third, etc)
- irregular verbs: 'aprire', 'chiúdere', 'chiédere', 'méttere', 'scrívere', 'pérdere', 'offrire'

CONVERSATION A

Dal droghiere / At the grocer's

Luisa is doing her daily shopping at the local grocer's, Dino.

DINO **Buongiorno signorina, desídera?**

LUISA **Vorrei due etti di prosciutto crudo e un bel pezzo di parmigiano.**

DINO **Il prosciutto è un po' di più, lascio così? E di parmigiano quanto ne vuole?**

LUISA **Me ne día tre, quattro etti. Ma parmigiano reggiano, mi raccomando!**

DINO **Certo, lo assaggi un po'. Buono eh! E desídera altro?**

LUISA **Ha la mozzarella?**

DINO **Sì, ce l'ho di búfala e di mucca.**

LUISA **Bene, ne prendo due di búfala.**

DINO **Éccole. Basta così?**

LUISA **Sì, per oggi si, quant'è?**

6

TRANSLATION A

DINO   Good morning, may I help you?

LUISA   I'd like 200 grammes of Parma ham and a large piece of Parmesan.

DINO   The ham is a bit over. Shall I leave it? And how much Parmesan would you like?

LUISA   Give me three or four hundred grammes. But I want the best Parmesan [from Reggio], mind!

DINO   Certainly, try it. Isn't it good? Anything else?

LUISA   Do you have any mozzarella?

DINO   Yes, I have mozzarella from buffalo's and cow's milk.

LUISA   Good, I'll take two buffalo ones.

DINO   Here they are. Is that all?

LUISA   Yes, for today. How much is it?

Exercise 52

Read Conversation A carefully, then answer the following questions:

1 Dove fa la spesa Luisa?
2 Quanto prosciutto compra?
3 Che parmigiano preferisce?
4 Quante mozzarelle compra?

41 THE PRONOUN 'NE'

Ne means:

1 'of it' or 'of them':

Quanto pane vuole? Ne voglio un chilo.
How much bread do you want? I want one kilo [of it].
Quanti amici inglesi ha? Ne ho molti.
How many English friends do you have? I have many [of them].

Quante pastine desídera? Ne vorrei tre.
How many little cakes do you want? I'd like three [of them].

Note that **ne** must not be omitted in Italian, while 'of it' and 'of them' are usually omitted in English.

2 'some' or 'any' when they are not followed by a noun:

Ha degli amici? Sì, ne ho.
Do you have any friends? Yes, I have some.
Ha del vino? No, non ne ho.
Do you have any wine? No, I don't have any.

3 'about it', 'about them':

Chi parla di política? Tutti ne párlano.
Who's talking about politics? Everyone's talking about it.

Exercise 53

Answer these questions using 'ne' and the expression given.
Examples:
Quanti francobolli vuole? ... 4→ Ne vorrei quattro.
Quanti fratelli ha? ... 1→ Ne ho uno.

1 Quanto olio vuole? ... un litro.
2 Quanto pane vuole? ... un chilo e mezzo.
3 Quante mozzarelle vuole? ... una sola.
4 Quanto salame vuole? ... 2 etti.
5 Quante arance vuole? ... 2 chili.
6 Quante mácchine ha? ... 1
7 Quanti figli ha? ... 4
8 Quante scarpe ha? Non ... molte.
9 Quanti soldi ha? ... pochi.
10 Quanto tempo ha? Non ...

OBJECT PRONOUNS WITH PERFECT TENSE

When you use direct object pronouns (me, her, etc) with the perfect tense, the past participle must agree (i.e. its ending changes in the same way as when it is used with **éssere**):

l'ho visto	I have seen him
l'ho vista	I have seen her
li ho visti	I have seen them (men or men and women)
le ho viste	I have seen them (women)
mi hai visto	you saw me (a man is talking)
mi hai vista	you saw me (a woman is talking)
vi ho visti	I saw you (several men and women or all men)
vi ho viste	I saw you (women)

Note that **li** and **le**, being plural, do not take the apostrophe. Note also that when the object pronoun is indirect – 'to me', 'to her' – the past participle does not change to agree with it.

Exercise 54

6

Answer the questions using 'lo', 'la', 'li' or 'le' and changing the ending of the past participles if necessary.
Examples:
Ha invitato María?→ Sì, l'ho invitata.
Avete comprato le pesche?→ Sì, le abbiamo comprate.

1 Ha invitato tutti gli amici?
2 Ha visitato la gallería?
3 Ha visitato il museo?
4 Ha portato i panini?
5 Ha mangiato le paste?
6 Avete invitato vostra suócera?
7 Avete guardato il catálogo?
8 Avete comprato le riviste?
9 Avete preso la mancia?
10 Avete visto Giovanni?

All' Oviesse

Luisa is buying some presents for her American friends at Oviesse (a department store) and asks the shop assistant, Carlo, for help with sizes.

LUISA **Vorrei un maglione di lana blù come questo, ma non sono sicura della misura.**

CARLO **È per Lei, signorina?**

LUISA **No, per un'amica americana. Porta il dodici negli Stati Uniti.**

CARLO **Attenda un áttimo che controllo. Dunque, il dieci corrisponde al quarantasei in Italia.**

LUISA **Grazie, allora glielo prendo e, scusi, dove sono le pantófole?**

CARLO **Da uomo o da donna?**

LUISA **Da uomo.**

CARLO **Il reparto calzature da uomo è al terzo piano. Sono anche queste per gli amici americani?**

LUISA **Sì, infatti le vorrei chiédere se sa anche le misure delle scarpe.**

CARLO **Sì, ce le ho qui. Il quarantadue italiano è l'equivalente dell'otto americano.**

LUISA **Il mio amico porta l'otto americano.**

CARLO **Allora chieda il quarantadue.**

LUISA **Mille grazie.**

TRANSLATION B

At the Oviesse department store

LUISA I'd like a blue woollen jumper like this one. But I am not sure about the size.

CARLO Is it for you?

LUISA No, for an American friend. She takes a 12 in the United States.

CARLO Wait a minute while I check. Right, size 12 is the equivalent of a size 46 in Italy.

LUISA Thank you, I'll get it for him. Where are the slippers please?

CARLO Men's or women's?

LUISA Men's.

CARLO The men's shoe department is on the 3rd floor. Are these for your American friends too?

LUISA Yes, in fact I'd like to ask you if you know about shoe sizes as well.

CARLO Yes, I have them here. The Italian 42 is the same as an American 8.

LUISA My friend takes an American 8.

CARLO Then ask for a 42.

LUISA Many thanks.

6

Exercise 55

Read Conversation B carefully, then answer these questions using complete sentences:

1 Che misura vuole Luisa per il maglione?
2 Di che colore lo preferisce?
3 A che piano sono le calzature da uomo?
4 Che misura di scarpe porta l'amico americano?
5 Per chi compra i regali Luisa?

43 DOUBLE PRONOUNS ('HE GIVES IT TO ME')

Very often in Italian you will find two pronouns together
before a verb where in English one would be enough:

Glielo prendo.	I take it (for him/her).
Me le mostra?	Will you show (them to) me?
Ce l'ho.	I have it.

Note that the direct object pronoun (**lo**, **la**, **li**, **le** and **ne**)
always follows the indirect one. The indirect object
pronouns also change their endings:

me
te
glie- ⎤
ce   ⎬ **lo, la, li, le, ne**
ve
glie- ⎦

Note also that **glielo**, **gliela**, **glieli**, **gliele**, **gliene** are
always written as one word, but all the other pronouns
are written as two separate words:

me la da	he gives it (a feminine object) to me
te li da	he gives them (masculine objects) to you (fam.)
ce lo da	he gives it (a masculine object) to us
ve le da	he gives them (feminine objects) to you (pl.)
glielo da	he gives it (masculine object) to you/to her/to him/to them

If these pronouns are followed by the perfect tense there
will be agreement (see section 42 above):

Glieli ho dati.	I have given them (i giornali) to him.
Te le ho scritte.	I have written them (le léttere) to you.

Exercise 56

Answer these questions addressed to you, using 'glielo', 'gliela', 'glieli', 'gliele' or 'gliene':

Examples:
Porta la rivista a María?→ Sì, gliela porto.
Porta il giornale a María?→ Sì, glielo porto.

1 Porta i panini ai ragazzi?
2 Scrive la léttera a María?
3 Dà il conto alla signora?
4 Dà i soldi alla signora?
5 Porta il vestito al signor Bianchi?
6 Scrive le léttere a tutti?
7 Compra la pasta per gli óspiti?
8 Compra i grissini per María?
9 Vende l'appartamento a questi signori?
10 Vende la casa a questi signori?

Exercise 57

Change the questions and answers in Exercise 56 into the perfect tense:

Examples:
Ha portato la rivista a María?→ Sì, gliel'ho portata.
Ha portato il giornale a María?→ Sì, gliel'ho portato.

6

Exercise 58

Answer these questions using the appropriate double pronouns.

Examples:

Chi Le ha fatto la spesa? ... il ragazzo. → Me l'ha fatta il ragazzo.

Chi vi ha offerto un aperitivo? ... María.→ Ce l'ha offerto María.

1 Chi Le ha consigliato questo ristorante? ... un'amica.
2 Chi Le ha dato l'indirizzo? ... il poliziotto.
3 Chi Le ha portato la valigia? ... il facchino.
4 Chi Le ha riparato l'orologio? ... l'orologiaio.
5 Chi Le ha mandato i fiori? ... un amico.
6 Chi vi ha portato l'antipasto? ... il cameriere.
7 Chi vi ha venduto le matite? ... la commessa.
8 Chi vi ha comprato quei regali? ... nostra figlia.
9 Chi vi ha prenotato l'albergo? ... l'agenzía.
10 Chi vi ha dato la moneta? ... l'impiegata.

Exercise 59a

Answer these questions addressed to you, using the formal 'Lei' form of the imperative and the appropriate double pronouns.

Example:

Glielo mando io?→ Sì, me lo mandi pure.
(Do I send it to you?)→ (Yes, send it to me.)

1 Glielo porto io?
2 Glieli mando io?
3 Gliele regalo io?
4 Gliela scrivo io?
5 Glielo prenoto io?

Exercise 59b

And now answer these questions, also addressed to you, by using the familiar 'tu' form of the imperative, imagining that you are talking to a friend.

Example:
Te lo porto io?→ Sì, pórtamelo pure!

1 Te la preparo io?
2 Te le mando io?
3 Te li compro io?
4 Te lo scrivo io?
5 Te la prendo io?

CONVERSATION C

Alla banca

Tony has used his credit card at the cashpoint outside the Banca del Lavoro in Verona but has not managed to get any money out, so he goes inside the bank to complain to the cashier:

TONY   Scusi, ho provato a usare la mia carta di crédito al Bancomát qui fuori, ma non sono riuscito a ritirare i soldi.

CASSIERE   Ha mai usato la Sua carta di crédito in Italia?

TONY   Sì, a Rímini e non ho mai avuto difficoltà.

CASSIERE   Mi dica cos'ha fatto.

TONY   Ho messo la carta dentro, poi ho digitato il mio códice segreto, ho premuto il tasto verde e ...

CASSIERE   E non ha funzionato?

TONY   Gliel'ho già detto. Sullo schermo c'è scritto che ho aspettato troppo e poi si è chiusa la grata e basta!

CASSIERE   Di sólito quando c'è scritto così è perchè ha dimenticato di prémere qualche tasto.

TONY **Ho capito. Allora, che cosa mi consiglia di fare?**

CASSIERE **Provi un'altra volta, ma stia attento e prema il tasto verde súbito.**

TONY **Va bene, ma se la mácchina non mi dà i soldi, me li può dare Lei?**

CASSIERE **Certo, non si preóccupi!**

TRANSLATION C

At the bank

TONY Excuse me, I tried to use my credit card at the automatic cashpoint outside, but I could not get the money out.

CASHIER Have you ever used your cashcard in Italy?

TONY Yes, in Rimini and I have never had any problems.

CASHIER Tell me what you did.

TONY I put my card in, then punched in my code number, pressed the green button and ...

CASHIER Did it not work, then?

TONY That's what I told you. On the screen it said that I had waited too long, then the shutter came down and that was it!

CASHIER Usually when it says that it is because you forgot to press some button.

TONY I see. What do you advise me to do?

CASHIER Try once more, but be careful and press the green button immediately.

TONY OK, but if the machine does not give me the money, can you do it?

CASHIER Yes, certainly!

6

44 ORDINAL NUMBERS (FIRST, SECOND, ETC)

Ordinal numbers are used in Italian in the same way as in English, with the exception of days of the month (see section 32). Study the first ten:

1st	**primo**	6th	**sesto**
2nd	**secondo**	7th	**séttimo**
3rd	**terzo**	8th	**ottavo**
4th	**quarto**	9th	**nono**
5th	**quinto**	10th	**décimo**

All other ordinal numbers are formed by removing the ending of the cardinal number and adding **-ésimo**:

11th	**undicésimo**
12th	**dodicésimo**
25th	**venticinquésimo**
1,000th	**millésimo**

Note that ordinal numbers have feminine and plural endings like all other adjectives ending in **-o**. Examples:

Te lo dico per la centésima volta.
I am telling you for the hundredth time.
Papa Giovanni Ventitreésimo
Pope John XXIII
il tredicésimo sécolo
the thirteenth century

6

Exercise 60

Translate the following sentences:

1 The shoe department is on the 10th floor.
2 This is the sixth week.
3 The 1st May is a national holiday in Italy.
4 We live in the twenty-first century.
5 Take (formal) the fourth street on your left.

IRREGULAR VERBS: 'APRIRE', 'CHIÉDERE', 'CHIÚDERE', 'MÉTTERE', ETC

The perfect tense of these verbs is formed in the usual way, by using the present tense of **avere** plus the past participle. But notice the latter's irregularity in each case:

	perfect tense
aprire (to open)	**ho aperto** (I opened)
chiédere (to ask)	**ho chiesto** (I asked)
chiúdere (to close)	**ho chiuso** (I closed)
méttere (to put)	**ho messo** (I put)
scrívere (to write)	**ho scritto** (I wrote)
pérdere (to lose)	**ho perso** (I lost)
offrire (to offer)	**ho offerto** (I offered)

Exercise 61

Read Conversation C carefully, then answer the following questions:

1 Dove ha messo la carta di crédito Tony?
2 Che cosa c'è scritto sullo schermo?
3 La grata del Bancomát è chiusa adesso?
4 Tony ha perso i soldi?
5 Perchè Tony è entrato in banca?

CONVERSATION D

Da Garda Moda / At the Garda Moda boutique

Jeff bought a shirt in a small boutique in Garda, but when he got back home he found that they had given him the wrong size. He asks the shop assistant ('Commessa') to change it.

JEFF	**Ho comprato questa camicia stamattina e vorrei cambiarla perchè è la taglia sbagliata.**
COMMESSA	**Ma non l'ha provata prima?**
JEFF	**No, ma ho chiesto il quarantadue e questo è il quaranta.**
COMMESSA	**Mi dispiace, signore, ma non abbiamo un quarantadue in quel colore.**
JEFF	**Allora mi può dare indietro i soldi?**
COMMESSA	**Vede, c'è scritto qui: 'Non si fanno rimborsi'. Ma Le posso dare un altro colore.**
JEFF	**No, è colpa vostra che mi avete dato la taglia sbagliata. Se non avete la mia taglia, voglio indietro i soldi.**
COMMESSA	**Guardi, teléfono all'altro nostro negozio e se neanche loro ce l'hanno, Le do un buono che può usare per qualsíasi artícolo.**
JEFF	**No, voglio i soldi o la camicia. Per favore, chiami il proprietario.**

6

TRANSLATION

JEFF	I bought this shirt this morning and I would like to change it because it is the wrong size.
SHOP ASSISTANT	Didn't you try it on first?
JEFF	I didn't, but I asked for a size 42 and this is a 40.
SHOP ASSISTANT	I am sorry, sir, but we don't have a 42 in that colour.
JEFF	Could I have my money back then?

SHOP ASSISTANT	Look, it says here: 'We don't give refunds.' But I could give you another colour.
JEFF	No, it is your fault, you gave me the wrong size. If you don't have my size I want my money back.
SHOP ASSISTANT	Look, I'll phone our other shop and if they don't have it either I'll give you a voucher which you can use to buy any other article.
JEFF	No, I want either the money or the shirt. Please call the owner.

Exercise 62

Put the following passage into the perfect tense, changing oggi into ieri and changing the endings of the past participles where necessary. Begin like this:
Ieri Tony e Luisa sono andati alla Rinascente ...

Oggi Tony e Luisa vanno alla Rinascente per comprare due regali: uno per la madre di Tony e l'altro per quella di Luisa. Luisa va al pianterreno, al reparto accessori, e compra una borsetta di pelle. Tony va a dare un'occhiata al reparto casalinghi al sesto piano. Guarda i servizi da tè e da caffè, ma non li compra.

Alle quattro Tony e Luisa vanno a préndere il tè a un bar in Piazza del Duomo e Luisa gli fa vedere la borsetta. Dopo due ore decídono di tornare alla Rinascente perchè Luisa vede che la cerniera della borsetta è rotta. La porta indietro all'Ufficio Reclami e chiede un rimborso dei soldi o un'altra borsetta. L'impiegato le domanda la ricevuta e dopo molte difficoltà le dà una borsetta nuova. Tony nel frattempo guarda dappertutto, ma non trova niente per la madre di Luisa.

Questo non è un pomeriggio molto fortunato per i due gióvani!

Me ne día due etti.
Perchè non gliele ha date?
Ho chiesto indietro i soldi.
Questa è la sesta settimana.

accessori (m. pl.)	accessories
aprire	to open
arancia (f.)	orange
artícolo (m.)	article
assaggiare	to taste
atténdere	to wait
áttimo (m.)	minute, moment
Bancomát	automatic cashpoint
basta	it is enough
blù	blue
borsetta (f.)	handbag
búfala (f.)	buffalo
buono (m.)	voucher
calzature (f. pl.)	footwear
cambiare	to change
camicia (f.)	shirt
capítolo (m.)	chapter
carta di crédito (f.)	credit card
cassiere (m.)	cashier
catálogo (m.)	catalogue
cerniera (f.)	zip
chiédere	to ask
chilo (m.)	kilo (gramme)
chiúdere	to close
códice segreto (m.)	PIN number
colore (m.)	colour
colpa (f.)	fault
come	like
comprare	to buy
conto (m.)	bill
corrispóndere (f.)	to be the equivalent of
dentro	inside
difficoltà (f.)	difficulty
digitare	to punch in

6

droghiere (m.)	grocer
etto (m.)	100 grammes
facchino (m.)	porter
festa (f.)	feast
fortunato	lucky
funzionare	to work, function
gióvane	young
grammo (m.)	gramme
grata (f.)	shutter
grissino (m.)	breadstick
impiegato/a (m./f.)	clerk
indietro	back
in tutto	altogether
lana (f.)	wool
léttera (f.)	letter
magazzino (m.)	store
maglione (m.)	sweater
mandare	to send
matita (f.)	pencil
méttere	to put
mi raccomando!	mind!
misura (f.)	size
moneta (f.)	loose change
mucca (f.)	cow
nazionale	national
nel frattempo	in the meantime
occhiata (f.)	look
olio (m.)	oil
orologiaio (m.)	watchmaker
pane (m.)	bread
panino (m.)	bread roll, sandwich
pantófole (f. pl.)	slippers
Papa (m.)	pope
parmigiano (m.)	Parmesan
pastina (f.)	little cake
pelle (f.)	leather
pérdere	to lose
pezzo (m.)	piece
piacévole	pleasant
política (f.)	politics
pomeriggio (m.)	afternoon

6

portare	to wear
portare indietro	to take back
prémere	to press
proprietario (m.)	owner
prosciutto (m.)	ham
reclami (m. pl.)	complaints
regalare	to give (as a present)
regalo (m.)	present
reparto (m.)	department
ricevuta (f.)	receipt
rimborso (m.)	refund
riparare	to mend
ritirare	to withdraw
riuscire	to succeed
rivista (f.)	magazine
rotto	broken
salame (m.)	salami
sbagliato	wrong
scarpe (f. pl.)	shoes
schermo (m.)	screen
sécolo (m.)	century
segreto	secret
servizio (m.)	set
soldi (m. pl.)	money
spéndere	to spend
spesa (f.)	shopping (for food)
spese (f. pl.)	purchases, shopping
stamattina	this morning
suócera (f.)	mother-in-law
taglia (f.)	size
tasto (m.)	button, key
usare	to use
vestito (m.)	dress, suit
visitare	to visit

6

Week 7

You will learn to:
- say how you feel and describe ailments
- report an accident
- name parts of the body

The grammar will include:
- reflexive verbs ('I enjoy myself')
- imperfect and pluperfect tenses ('I was doing', 'I had done')
- irregular plurals
- irregular verbs: 'córrere', 'rimanere', 'rispóndere', 'rómpere', 'sedersi', 'succédere'

CONVERSATION A

In ambulatorio

Tony Jones has gone to Dr Guglielmini with severe stomachache:

DOTTORE **Si accómodi, signor Jones. Come si sente?**

TONY **Ho mal di stómaco da due giorni e mi fa veramente male.**

DOTTORE **Dov'è il dolore di preciso?**

TONY **Qui, proprio in alto, e non mi passa neanche se mi córico.**

DOTTORE **Si metta sul lettino che La vísito. [Dopo la visita]**

DOTTORE **Bene, si vesta e si sieda qui che Le spiego.**

TONY **Allora, cosa ne pensa?**

DOTTORE **Secondo me, Lei ha una forma leggera di gastroenterite.**

TONY **Ma è una malattía seria!**

DOTTORE **Non si preóccupi, prenda questa medicina tre volte al giorno dopo i pasti per una settimana e poi torni da me.**

TONY **Grazie.**

DOTTORE **Prego, e non si preóccupi!**

At the doctor's surgery

DOCTOR Sit down, Mr Jones. How do you feel?

TONY I've had stomachache for two days and it is really painful.

DOCTOR Where exactly is the pain?

TONY High up here and it doesn't go even when I lie down.

DOCTOR Lie on the couch and I will examine you.
[After the examination]

DOCTOR Right, get dressed and come and sit down while I explain.

TONY Well, what do you think (about it)?

DOCTOR In my opinion you have a mild form of gastroenteritis.

TONY But that is a serious illness!

DOCTOR Don't worry, take this medicine three times a day after meals for a week and then come back to see me.

TONY Thank you.

DOCTOR You're welcome, and don't worry!

7

46 REFLEXIVE VERBS ('I ENJOY MYSELF')

In Italian reflexive verbs (like 'I enjoy myself', 'I dress myself', etc) are much more common than in English. They include:

1 Verbs that are reflexive in both languages:

divertirsi	to enjoy oneself
farsi male	to hurt oneself
lavarsi	to wash oneself
vestirsi	to dress oneself

2 Verbs that are reflexive in Italian but not in English:

addormentarsi	to fall asleep
alzarsi	to get up
ammalarsi	to fall ill
chiamarsi	to be called
coricarsi	to lie down
dimenticarsi	to forget
ricordarsi	to remember
riposarsi	to rest
sedersi	to sit down
svegliarsi	to wake up

… including many verbs which in English start with 'to get …':

annoiarsi	to get bored
arrabbiarsi	to get angry
pérdersi	to get lost
preoccuparsi	to get worried/to worry
sposarsi	to get married
stancarsi	to get tired
svestirsi	to get undressed

7

All reflexive verbs are preceded by the following reflexive pronouns:

present tense

mi lavo	I wash myself
ti lavi	you wash yourself
si lava	he washes himself/she washes herself/you (form.) wash yourself
ci laviamo	we wash ourselves
vi lavate	you wash yourselves
si lávano	they wash themselves

All reflexive verbs take **éssere** in the perfect tense and the past participle agrees with the reflexive pronoun:

perfect tense

mi sono lavato/a	I washed myself
ti sei lavato/a	you washed yourself
si è lavato/a	he washed himself/she washed herself/you (form.) washed yourself
ci siamo lavati/e	we washed ourselves
vi siete lavati/e	you washed yourselves
si sono lavati/e	they washed themselves

Note that the reflexive pronouns must always be expressed in Italian, even when the verb is followed by a direct object:

Ci siamo lavati.
We washed
Mi sono lavato le mani.
I washed my hands.
Si è fatta male al ginocchio.
She hurt her knee.

Note also that the definite article, not the possessive adjective, is then used with the part of the body.

7

Exercise 63

Read Conversation A carefully, then answer the following questions:

1 Perchè Tony va dal dottore?
2 Secondo Lei, Tony si preóccupa molto?
3 Quante volte al giorno deve préndere la medicina?
4 Quando deve tornare dal dottore?
5 Tony ha una malattía seria?

Exercise 64

Answer these questions addressed to you, using the reflexive verb and the expression given.

Example:
Quando si rade? ... ogni mattina.→ Mi rado ogni mattina.
(When do you shave?) ... (every morning.)→ (I shave every morning.)

1	Quando si alza ?	... alle 8.
2	Quando si córica?	... alle 11.
3	Quando si lava?	... tutte le mattine.
4	Quando si stanca?	... a lavorare troppo.
5	Quando si arrabbia?	Non ... mai.
6	Quando si annoia?	... a far la coda.
7	Quando si diverte?	... in vacanza.
8	Quando si sveglia?	... alle 7.30.
9	Quando si riposa?	... dopo pranzo.
10	Quando si perde?	... se non ho la cartina.

7

Exercise 65

Complete the following sentences using these verbs:

addormentarsi   to fall asleep
farsi male   to get hurt
sentirsi bene   to feel well
sentirsi male   to feel ill
ricordarsi   to remember
dimenticarsi   to forget
sposarsi   to get married
ammalarsi   to fall ill
lavarsi   to wash
asciugarsi   to dry oneself

Make sure that you use the same person and tense as in the first part of the sentence.
Examples:
Se siamo stanchi …→ Se siamo stanchi ci riposiamo.

Quando ho lavorato per 10 ore …→ Quando ho lavorato per 10 ore mi sono stancato/a.

1 Quando cado …
2 Quando sono andati a letto
3 Ieri è andata dal dottore perchè …
4 María è stata a letto quando …
5 Abbiamo fatto il bagno, poi …
6 Non ti ho telefonato perchè …
7 María e Giovanni sono andati in chiesa e …
8 Non prendo più le medicine perchè …
9 Quando sono sporchi …
10 Se scrivo la lista della spesa …

7

Un incidente stradale

Peter describes to his girlfriend Luisa a road accident he saw in the centre of Rome:

PETER **Scúsami per il ritardo, ma c'è stato un brutto incidente davanti all'università.**

LUISA **Un incidente? Cos'è successo?**

PETER **Mentre aspettavo l'áutobus ho visto un mio compagno che è stato investito da un motorino.**

LUISA **Il tuo compagno attraversava la strada?**

PETER **Sì, ha visto l'áutobus arrivare e si è messo a córrere, ma c'era un motorino che veniva da una strada laterale e lui non se n'è accorto.**

LUISA **Mamma mia, si è fatto male?**

PETER **Ho proprio paura di sì, io sono corso súbito per aiutarlo. Forse si è rotto una gamba.**

LUISA **Avete chiamato l'ambulanza?**

PETER **Sì, ed è venuta súbito. L'hanno portato al Pronto Soccorso dell'ospedale.**

LUISA **Se vuoi, possiamo andare a trovarlo oggi pomeriggio.**

7

A road accident

PETER I'm sorry I'm late but there has been a terrible accident opposite the university.

LUISA An accident? What happened?

PETER While I was waiting for the bus I saw one of my friends being run over by a scooter.

LUISA Was your friend crossing the road?

PETER Yes, he saw the bus coming and he started running, but there was a scooter coming from a side street and he didn't notice it.

LUISA Oh dear! Was he hurt?

PETER He may have broken his leg.

LUISA Did you call an ambulance?

PETER Yes, and it came immediately. They have taken him to A & E at the hospital.

LUISA If you like we could go and visit him this afternoon.

Exercise 66

Read Conversation B, then answer the following questions:

7

1 Perchè Peter è in ritardo?

2 Che cosa è successo al suo compagno?

3 Perchè il suo compagno non ha visto il motorino?

4 Dove l'hanno portato?

5 Dov'era Peter quando è successo tutto questo?

47 IMPERFECT TENSE ('I WAS DOING')

The endings of the imperfect tense are formed by removing **-re** from the infinitive and adding **-vo**, **-vi**, **-va**, **-vamo**, **-vate**, **-vano**:

parlare	vedere	venire
parlavo	vedevo	venivo
parlavi	vedevi	venivi
parlava	vedeva	veniva
parlavamo	vedevamo	venivamo
parlavate	vedevate	venivate
parlávano	vedévano	venívano

When talking about something which happened in the past you use the imperfect tense:

1 to describe people or things:

Garibaldi aveva la barba.
Garibaldi had a beard.

2 to describe habitual or continuous action, as in English 'I used to do' or 'I was doing':

María mangiava quando sono arrivato.
Mary was eating when I arrived.
Da píccola abitavo in campagna.
As a child I used to live in the country.

3 to describe something that happened in the past and went on for an unspecified period of time:

I bambini non volévano uscire.
The children did not want to go out.

48 | USE OF PERFECT AND IMPERFECT TENSES

To help you with the use of these two past tenses,
remember: the perfect is used when the action
happened in the past and is over with, the imperfect is
used when the action went on for an unspecified period
of time:

**Ho mandato una léttera a María perchè non stava
bene.**

ho mandato:	The action is over and done with.
stava:	Mary was unwell for an unspecified period of time.

49 | IMPERFECT OF 'ÉSSERE'

ero	I was
eri	you were
era	he/she was
eravamo	we were
eravate	you were
érano	they were

7

Exercise 67

Answer these questions addressed to you, using the imperfect tense: Examples:

Andava a scuola quando era píccolo/a?→ Sì, andavo a scuola quando ero píccola/o.

Andavate a scuola quando eravate píccoli?→ Sì, andavamo a scuola quando eravamo píccoli.

1 Studiava quando era píccolo?
2 Faceva molti sport quando era a scuola?
3 Viaggiava molto quando abitava in Italia?
4 Andava sempre in mácchina quando lavorava in centro?
5 Sentiva molto i rumori quando dormiva al pianterreno?
6 Facevate molte gite quando eravate in montagna?
7 Andavate fuori spesso quando abitavate a Milano?
8 Fumavate quando avevate 18 anni?
9 Mangiavate solo verdura quando vivevate in Inghilterra?
10 Compravate sempre il giornale quando lavoravate in Italia?

7

Exercise 68

Answer the following questions using 'ero' or 'eravamo' and the expressions given. Examples:

Perchè non è venuto ieri? ... impegnato.→ Perchè ero impegnato.

(Why didn't you come yesterday?)→ (Because I was busy.)

Perchè non siete venuti ieri? ... impegnati.→ Perchè eravamo impegnati.

1 Perchè è andato all'ospedale? ... malato.
2 Perchè non ha scritto? ... indisposto.
3 Perchè non ha telefonato? ... arrabbiato.
4 Perchè non è venuto prima? ... troppo stanco.
5 Perchè non ha visto il motorino? ... distratto.
6 Perchè non avete preso il caffè? ... senza soldi.
7 Perchè siete andati dal dottore? ... malati.
8 Perchè non siete venuti? ... stanchi.
9 Perchè non vi siete fermati di più? ... in ritardo.
10 Perchè avete chiamato l'ambulanza? ... molto preoccupati.

Exercise 69

Change the following sentences into the imperfect tense and make a contrast. Example:

Adesso non leggo più.→ Una volta leggevo molto.

(Now I don't read any more.)→ (Once I used to read a lot.)

1 Adesso non viaggiate più.
2 Adesso non ci preoccupiamo più.
3 Adesso non viàggiano più.
4 Adesso non scrivi più.
5 Adesso non lavora più.
6 Adesso non mi diverto più.
7 Adesso non usciamo più.
8 Adesso non fumo più.
9 Adesso non leggi più.
10 Adesso non pàrlano più.

Exercise 70

Put these sentences into the past tense, using 'ieri', making sure that you use both the perfect and imperfect tenses where necessary. Example:

Prende un'aspirina perchè non si sente bene.→ Ieri ha preso un'aspirina perchè non si sentiva bene.

1 Prendo l'áutobus perchè sono stanca.

2 Non guardo la televisione perchè non funziona.

3 Sono a Firenze e vado agli Uffizi.

4 Noi andiamo dal dottore perchè abbiamo la febbre.

5 Il dottore ti vísita in casa quando sei a letto malata.

6 Mi alzo alle dieci perchè è festa.

7 Mentre leggo il giornale entra il mio óspite.

8 Mentre scrivo la léttera i bambini mángiano tutti i cioccolatini.

9 Sandra ha mal di testa e non va a lavorare.

10 Mentre cammino lungo la strada vedo un incidente.

50 IRREGULAR PLURALS

PARTS OF THE BODY

When describing parts of the body take care because many have irregular plurals and some also change from masculine to feminine:

l'orecchio (m.)	le orecchie (f.)	ears
il labbro (m.)	le labbra (f.)	lips
il braccio (m.)	le braccia (f.)	arms
il dito (m.)	le dita (f.)	fingers
il ginocchio (m.)	le ginocchia (f.)	knees
la mano (f.)	le mani (f.)	hands

Examples:
Giovanni si è fatto male alle ginocchia.
John hurt his knees.
Ho le dita gelate.
My fingers are frozen.

Note that you must use the definite article with parts of the body (see note at the end of section 46).

MORE IRREGULAR PLURALS

Other irregular plurals include the following:

1 Masculine words ending in **-a** change this to **-i** in the plural:

il programma	i programmi
il telegramma	i telegrammi
l'artista	gli artisti
il pianista	i pianisti
il violinista	i violinisti

2 Foreign words, words ending with an accented vowel, words ending in **-i** and abbreviated words remain unchanged in the plural:

la città	le città
la difficoltà	le difflcoltà
l'hobby	gli hobby
il taxi	i taxi
la tesi (thesis)	le tesi
il bar	i bar
il caffè	i caffè
la radio	le radio

7

CONVERSATION C

In farmacia

Jeff is asking the chemist or farmacista for advice after getting badly burnt by the sun.

FARMACISTA **Desídera?**

JEFF **Vorrei una crema contro le scottature.**

FARMACISTA **Si è proprio preso una bella scottatura al viso.**

JEFF **Non solo al viso, ma anche sulla schiena e sulle gambe.**

FARMACISTA **Le do questo pomata. Se la metta due volte al giorno, ma stia attento a non esporsi al sole.**

JEFF **Va bene, grazie. E quanto devo evitare il sole?**

FARMACISTA **Finchè l'arrossamento non è passato. Se poi si spella torni da me che Le do un'altra pomata protettiva.**

JEFF **Grazie mille, dottoressa.**

TRANSLATION C

At the chemist's

CHEMIST May I help you?

JEFF I'd like something for sunburn.

CHEMIST You've certainly burnt your face badly.

JEFF Not only my face but my back and legs too.

CHEMIST I can give you this cream. Apply twice a day, but do be careful and don't sunbathe.

JEFF All right, thank you. How long should I stay away from the sun?

CHEMIST Until all the redness has gone. Then if you start peeling come back and I'll give you another protective cream.

JEFF Thank you, doctor.

Exercise 71

Read Conversation C carefully, then answer these questions:

1 Perchè Jeff va dalla farmacista?
2 Che cosa gli prescrive?
3 Dove si deve méttere la pomata?
4 Fino a quando deve evitare il sole?
5 Poi che cosa deve fare?

Exercise 72

Complete the following conversation using the clues given:

YOU   Buongiorno, dottore.

DOCTOR Buongiorno, si accomodi. Che disturbi ha?

YOU   (I have a backache.)

DOCTOR Da quanto tempo ha questi síntomi?

YOU   (For two days.)

DOCTOR Vediamo. Si córichi sul lettino e mi dica
       se Le fa male.

YOU   (Yes it is very painful. Is it serious?)

DOCTOR No, non si preóccupi! Dovrebbe éssere solo
       uno strappo muscolare.

YOU   (What is a 'muscle strain'? What shall I do?)

DOCTOR Uno strappo muscolare è abbastanza comune.
       Si riposi il più possíbile e se deve piegarsi,
       pieghi le ginocchia e non la schiena.

YOU   (Could you give me something to (per) sleep?)

DOCTOR Le do questa medicina per rilassare i múscoli.

YOU   (Thank you, doctor!)

51 MORE IRREGULAR VERBS

Have a look at the present tense of **sedersi** (to sit down), then notice the perfect tense of some other irregular verbs; some are formed with the present tense of **avere**, others with the present tense of **éssere** (see week 3, section 23 if you need reminding about this).

present tense of **sedersi**
mi siedo
ti siedi
si siede
ci sediamo
vi sedete
si siédono

		perfect tense
córrere	to run	**sono corso**
rimanere	to stay	**sono rimasto/a**
rispóndere	to reply	**ho risposto**
rómpere	to break	**ho rotto**
succédere	to happen	**è successo** (it happened)

52 PLUPERFECT ('I HAD DONE')

7

This tense ('I had seen', 'I had gone') is used in Italian as it is in English – to express an action that happened before another action in the past. It is formed by using the imperfect tense of the verbs **avere** and **éssere** and the past participle:

Avevo già chiamato l'ambulanza quando sei arrivato tu.
I had already called an ambulance when you arrived.
Non era ancora andata a trovarlo.
She had not gone to see him yet.

Exercise 73

Put the verbs in brackets into the pluperfect in the following sentences.

Example:

Ieri Anna (andare) dal signor Bianchi, così io sono rimasta sola.→ Ieri Anna era andata dal signor Bianchi, così io sono rimasta sola.

1 Eva non (rispóndere) alla mia léttera, così non le ho più scritto.

2 Gli studenti (andare) a Firenze due altre volte, ma questa volta hanno visto gli Uffizi.

3 Voi (éssere) in casa tutto il tempo e non me l'avete detto?

4 Il dottore (scrívere) la ricetta lunedì, ma l'ho ricevuta oggi.

5 María non (rómpere) mai niente, ma oggi ha fatto un disastro!

6 Silvio (farsi male) al braccio, così non è potuto venire.

7 Che cosa (succédere), perchè non sei andato?

8 La mácchina si è fermata perchè io non ci (méttere) benzina.

9 Ha detto che (chiúdere) la porta.

10 Noi (sedersi) già, quando sei entrato tu.

Non è venuto perchè era stanco.
Si sono fatti male alle braccia.
Tony ha detto che il motorino l'aveva investito.
Tutti i taxi érano occupati.

addormentarsi	to fall asleep
ambulanza (f.)	ambulance
ambulatorio (m.)	surgery
aiutare	to help
accórgersene	to notice
alzarsi	to get up
ammalarsi	to fall ill
annoiarsi	to get bored
artista (m. & f.)	artist
asciugarsi	to get dry
arrabbiarsi	to get angry
arrabbiato	angry
arrossamento (m.)	reddening
attraversare	to cross
aver male di	to have a pain in ...
barba (f.)	beard
benzina (f.)	petrol
braccio (m.) (pl. -a f.)	arm
brutto	ugly
camminare	to walk
campagna (f.)	countryside
chiamarsi	to call oneself, to be called
cioccolatini (m. pl.)	chocolates
compagno	friend, mate
coricarsi	to lie down
córrere	to run
crema (f.)	cream
di preciso	exactly
distratto	absent-minded, distracted
dito (m.) (pl. -a f.)	finger, toe
divertirsi	to enjoy oneself
dottore (m.)	doctor
esporsi al sole	to sunbathe
evitare	to avoid

finchè ... non	until
farmacista (m. & f.)	chemist
far male	to hurt
febbre (f.)	fever, temperature
festa (f.)	feast (day), holiday
forma (f.)	form
forse	perhaps
gamba (f.)	leg
gastroenterite (f.)	gastroenteritis
gelato	frozen
ginocchio (m.) (pl. -a f.)	knee
hobby (m.)	hobby
impegnato	busy, engaged
incidente (m.)	accident
indisposto	indisposed, unwell
investire	to run over
labbro (m.) (pl. -a f.)	lip
laterale	on the side
lavarsi	to wash oneself
leggero	light, mild
letto (m.)	bed
lettino (m.)	couch
malattía (f.)	illness, disease
male (m.) (di ...)	ache, pain
mano (m.) (pl. -i f.)	hand
medicina (f.)	medicine
médico (m.)	medical doctor
médico	medical
motorino (m.)	scooter
orecchio (m.) (pl. -e f.)	ear
ospedale (m.)	hospital
passare	to pass, to go
pérdersi	to get lost
pianista (m. & f.)	pianist
pomata (f.)	ointment
preoccuparsi	to worry
preoccupato	worried
prescrívere	to prescribe
programma (m.)	programme
Pronto Soccorso (m.)	A & E
protettivo	protective

7

rádersi	to shave
ricetta (f.)	prescription
rimanere	to stay
riposarsi	to rest
rómpere	to break
schiena (f.)	back
scottatura (f.)	burn
secondo	according to, in the opinion of
sedersi	to sit down
sentirsi	to feel
serio	serious
sole (m.)	sun
spellarsi	to peel
spiegare	to explain
sporcarsi	to get dirty
sporco	dirty
sposarsi	to get married
stancarsi	to get tired
stómaco (m.)	stomach
strada (f.)	road
strappo muscolare (m.)	muscular sprain
súbito	immediately
succédere	to happen
svegliarsi	to wake up
svestirsi	to undress
telegramma (m.)	telegramme
testa (f.)	head
una volta	once
uscire	to go out
vestirsi	to get dressed
violinista (m. & f.)	violinist
vísita (f.)	visit, examination
visitare	to visit, to examine
viso (m.)	face

7

Week 8

You will learn to:
- talk about hobbies and interests
- express opinions on TV, cinema, and theatre
- arrange meetings and activities
- agree or disagree and apologise
- write a letter

The grammar will include:
- comparatives and superlatives (more, most, less, least, as)
- prepositions followed by infinitives
- expressions using 'avere'
- agreement and disagreement
- use of the verb 'fare'
- irregular verb: 'accórgersi'

CONVERSATION A

Alla festa

Fabio and Marina are at a party, where they have just been introduced, and discuss their mutual interests.

FABIO **Le piace il calcio?**

MARINA **No, non mi interesso di sport, e Lei?**

FABIO **Beh, sono un tifoso dell'Inter, ma la mia vera passione è la lírica.**

MARINA **Ma davvero? Anche a me piace molto. Specialmente Puccini.**

FABIO **Qual è il Suo cantante preferito?**

MARINA **Per me Plácido Domingo è insuperábile. Ma anche Pavarotti è bravo, intendiámoci.**

FABIO **Bravo? È único! È il miglior tenore del mondo.**

MARINA **In un certo senso, sì. Tecnicamente è bravíssimo. Ma Domingo ha una voce più calda, più espressiva.**

FABIO **In questo Le do ragione. Domingo è molto espressivo e anche récita bene. Ma ha visto Pavarotti alla televisione ieri?**

MARINA **Sì, per dire la verità, mi è piaciuto.**
FABIO **Vede? Gliel'ho detto che è un genio!**

TRANSLATION A

At the party

FABIO Do you like football?
MARINA No, I'm not interested in sports, and you?
FABIO Well, I am a fan of Inter Milan but opera is my real passion.
MARINA Really? I like it very much too. Specially Puccini.
FABIO Who is your favourite singer?
MARINA For me, Placido Domingo is unbeatable. But Pavarotti is good too, I admit.
FABIO Good? He is unique! He is the best tenor in the world.
MARINA In a way, yes. Technically he is very good. But Domingo's voice has more feeling, more warmth.
FABIO I agree with you about that. Domingo sings with feeling and acts well too. But did you see Pavarotti on TV yesterday?
MARINA Yes, I must admit, I liked him.
FABIO See? Didn't I tell you that he is a genius!

8

53 COMPARATIVES (MORE, LESS, AS)

COMPARATIVES OF INEQUALITY: 'MORE/LESS ... THAN'

In Italian, when you compare two things which are unequal you use **più** (more) or **meno** (less) in front of the adjective or adverb:

Ha una voce più espressiva.
He has a more expressive voice.

È una strada meno affollata.
It is a less crowded street.
Guardo la televisione più spesso.
I watch television more often.

'Than' is translated by:

1 di before a noun, pronoun or numeral:

Il film dura meno di un'ora.
The film lasts less than one hour.
Tutti si divértono più di me.
They all enjoy themselves more than I.
Capisco María più facilmente di Gino.
I understand Mary more easily than Gino.

2 che before any other part of speech:

Questa storia è più trágica che cómica.
This story is more tragic than comic.
Vado a teatro più spesso d'inverno che d'estate.
I go to the theatre more often in winter than in summer.

Note that if two similar things with different qualities are being compared you use **che** even before nouns:

Ci sono più turisti che veronesi in città.
There are more tourists than Veronese in town.
Leggo più riviste che giornali.
I read more magazines than newspapers.

8

COMPARATIVES OF EQUALITY: 'AS ... AS'
When comparing two things that are alike ('as ... as'), in Italian you don't translate the first 'as' and you use **come** to translate the second:

Milano è grande come Roma.
Milan is as big as Rome.

Milano non è grande come Londra.
Milan is not as big as London.

Note that when in English you use 'as much' or 'as many', in Italian you use **tanto … quanto**, but these agree with the noun or pronoun they refer to:

Ho tanto tempo quanto te.
I have as much time as you.

Ho tanti amici quanti te.
or
Ho tanti amici quanto te.
I have as many friends as you.

Exercise 74

Read Conversation A again very carefully, then answer these questions:

1 Secondo Marina, Pavarotti è bravo come Domingo?
2 Perchè Fabio non è d'accordo?
3 Tecnicamente, chi canta meglio?
4 A Marina è piaciuto Pavarotti alla televisione?
5 Marina è appassionata di sport?
6 Per chi fa il tifo Fabio?

8

Exercise 75

Fill in the gaps in the following sentences using 'più di' or 'più che'. Example:
Luisa guadagna ... ... 600 euro al mese.→ Luisa guadagna più di seicento euro al mese.

1 Ci sono ... ... 30.000 spettatori all'Arena.
2 Secondo me Roma è ... grande ... Milano.
3 Giovanni è ... studioso ... intelligente.
4 Ci sono ... teatri a Roma ... a Torino.
5 Conosco ... attori italiani ... stranieri.
6 Sua figlia è ... alta ...lei.
7 Fa ... caldo in Italia ... in Inghilterra.
8 Parla ... piano ... me.
9 Luisa mangia ... ... tutti.
10 L'Aida mi piace ... ... Rigoletto.

54 SUPERLATIVES (MOST, LEAST)

In Italian you form the superlative by putting **il più**, **la più**, **i più**, **le più** ('the most' or '-est' in English) in front of the adjective:

Il Pánteon ha la più grande cúpola del mondo.
The Pantheon has the largest dome in the world.

NOTE: English 'in' is translated by **di** after a superlative.

SUPERLATIVES ENDING IN -ÍSSIMO

To say that something is very big, very easy etc in Italian you can either use **molto** or add **-íssimo/a/i/e** at the end of the adjective:

This opera is very long.
or

Quest'ópera è molto lunga.
Quest'ópera è lunghíssima.

The palaces are very old.
or

I palazzi sono molto vecchi.
I palazzi sono vecchíssimi.

55 IRREGULAR COMPARATIVES AND SUPERLATIVES

buono	**migliore**	**óttimo**
good	better/best	very good
cattivo	**peggiore**	**péssimo**
bad	worse/worst	very bad
grande	**maggiore**	**mássimo**
great	greater/greatest	very great
píccolo	**minore**	**mínimo**
small	smaller/smallest	very small

molto	much	**più**	more/most
poco	a little	**meno**	less/least
bene	well	**meglio**	better*
male	badly	**peggio**	worse*

* These are only used as adverbs.

Examples:

'Zia Teresa' è il miglior ristorante di Nápoli.
'Zia Teresa' is the best restaurant in Naples.
Il Barolo è un óttimo vino.
Barolo is a very good wine.
I miei fratelli minori sono a scuola.
My younger brothers are at school.
Canta meglio di me.
He sings better than I.

Note that **minore** also means 'younger' and **maggiore** 'older'.

Note also that **migliore** can drop the final **e** when followed by another word. The same is true of many other Italian words that end in **-re**:

È il peggior film del festival.
It is the worst film in the festival.
Penso di andár via.
I am thinking of leaving.
Parlo al signor Rossi.
I am speaking to Mr Rossi.

Exercise 76

Translate the following sentences:

1 This is the worst wine in the world!

2 We are as good as you (pl.) in Italian.

3 There were more than 20,000 spectators.

4 María Callas was a very famous singer.

5 St Paul's (Cathedral) is not as big as St Peter's.

6 John drinks more wine than water.

7 I feel better now.

8 These programmes are very boring.

9 We did not buy as many presents as you (pl.).

10 My younger sister lives in Milan.

CONVERSATION B

In Piazza San Marco

Tony and Luisa have come to Venice for the day. Luisa wants to visit a church with her friend Carla and Tony wants to go to an exhibition.

TONY **Allora, se vuoi andare alla Chiesa del Cármine con Carla io mi fermo a vedere la mostra.**

LUISA **Poi dove ci troviamo?**

TONY **Fra due ore davanti all'Accademia?**

LUISA **Va bene.**
[Due ore dopo]

LUISA **Éccoci qua, ti è piaciuta la mostra?**

TONY **Sì, moltíssimo. E voi, vi siete divertite?**

LUISA **Sì. L'Assunzione del Tiziano era magnífica. Poi, per strada, abbiamo fatto anche delle cómpere.**

TONY **Davvero? Cosa avete comprato?**

LUISA **Dei regali per i nostri amici.**

TONY **Bene. Ma non avete fame adesso?**

LUISA **Sì, molto. Abbiamo visto una trattoria qui vicino, perchè non ci andiamo insieme?**

TONY **Volentieri. Ho proprio voglia di sedermi e riposarmi un po'.**

LUISA **Óttima idea. Andiamo!**

TRANSLATION B

In St Mark's Square

TONY If you want to go and see the Chiesa del Carmine with Carla I'll stay and see the exhibition.

LUISA Where shall we meet* afterwards?

TONY In two hours in front of the Accademia?

LUISA OK.
[Two hours later]

LUISA Here we are, did you like the exhibition?

TONY Yes, very much. And you, did you enjoy yourselves?

LUISA Yes, Titian's Assumption was marvellous. Then on the way we went and did some shopping.

TONY Did you? What did you buy?

LUISA Some presents for our friends.

TONY Good. Are you hungry now?

LUISA Yes, very. We saw a 'trattoria' near here, why don't we go there together?

TONY I'd love to. I do feel like sitting down and resting for a while.

LUISA Excellent idea! Let's go!

* The verb 'to meet' is translated by **trovarsi** to describe an arranged meeting and by **incontrarsi** to describe a chance meeting.

8

Exercise 77

Read Conversation B carefully, then answer the following questions:

1 Che cosa vuole vedere Tony?

2 Perchè non ci va anche Luisa?

3 Dove si tróvano fra due ore?

4 Che cosa hanno comprato le due ragazze?

5 Dove vanno a mangiare?

56 PREPOSITIONS WITH INFINITIVES

In Italian 'to' before an infinitive is:

1 Not translated with modal verbs, such as **voglio, posso, devo** and **preferisco, mi piace, desídero:**

Preferisco stare a casa.
I prefer to stay at home.
Non mi piace camminare.
I don't like to walk.

2 Translated by **a** with verbs such as **andare, venire, restare, imparare, divertirsi, riuscire:**

Vado a vedere la mostra.
I am going to see the exhibition.
Comincio a capire.
I am beginning to understand.
Li invito a mangiare.
I invite them to eat.

3 Translated by **di** with verbs such as **finire, pensare, crédere, accórgersi, prométtere, decídere, sperare:**

Ha deciso di venire.
He decided to come.

8

Finisco di léggere.
I finish reading.
Penso di venire.
I am thinking of coming.

Note that in English verbs preceded by prepositions end in '-ing', but in Italian only the infinitive can be used:

Ha cominciato a criticare.
He started criticizing.

Note also that there is no rule that will help you decide which verbs take **a** and which **di**. Try to memorize them, or write them down whenever you see or hear them being used.

Exercise 78

Complete the following sentences with the verbs given, making sure that you use the correct prepositions, if required, before the infinitive:

1 María e Gianni (decided to) non uscire oggi.
2 (we start) camminare alle tre.
3 (she hopes) arrivare in tempo.
4 (I don't like) guardare la partita di calcio.
5 (do you enjoy) (formal) visitare i musei e le galleríe?
6 (he prefers) fare le cómpere.
7 Tutti i negozi (must) chiúdere una volta alla settimana.
8 (I finished) scrívere la léttera.
9 (they think) capire molto ma non capíscono niente.
10 (we are going) mangiare al ristorante.

8

57 APOLOGISING

To say that you are sorry, in Italian, you use **dispiacere**:

mi dispiace	I am sorry
ti dispiace	you are sorry
gli dispiace	he is sorry
le dispiace	she is sorry
Le dispiace	you are sorry (form.)
ci dispiace	we are sorry
gli dispiace	they are sorry

Mi dispiace, ma non posso fermarmi.
I am sorry but I can't stay.
Ci dispiace di éssere in ritardo.
We are sorry we're late.

LETTER-WRITING PRACTICE

Tony is writing to his teacher to apologize for not attending his classes.

Venezia, 24 settembre '02

Caro Professore,

Sono venuto a Venezia con la mia ragazza e avevamo pensato di tornare doménica sera. Purtroppo, però, non possiamo arrivare in tempo per la lezione d'italiano lunedì perchè la nostra amica ci ha gentilmente invitati a restare qui ancora per qualche giorno per vedere la Regata stórica.

Abbiamo deciso di accettare perchè non vogliamo pérdere l'occasione di vedere uno spettácolo único al mondo come questo. La prego di accettare le mie scuse per questa assenza.

8

Mi dispiace molto di dovér pérdere le lezioni e vorrei pregarLa di tenermi i fogli delle lezioni di lunedì, se questo non Le è di troppo disturbo.

Distinti saluti

Tony Smith

TRANSLATION

Venice, 24th September '02

Dear Professor,

I came to Venice with my girlfriend and we had thought of coming back on Sunday night. Unfortunately, however, we cannot be back in time for the Italian lesson on Monday because our friend has kindly invited us to stay here for a few days to see the historic Regatta.

We have decided to accept because we do not want to miss the opportunity to see such a unique spectacle [in the world]. Please accept my apology for this absence.

I am very sorry to have to miss classes and may I ask you to keep Monday's worksheets for me if it is not too much trouble for you.

Yours sincerely,

Tony Smith

NOTE: a formal letter usually starts with **Caro** (or **Egregio**), **Cara** (or **Gentile**) followed by the addressee's title (**Dottore, Signore, Dottoressa** etc) and ends with **Distinti saluti** (Yours faithfully/sincerely). A less formal letter starts with **Caro/Cara** followed by the addressee's first name and ends with **Tanti saluti** or **Affettuosi saluti** (Love, Much love). The address is usually put at the bottom of a letter.

8

Exercise 79

Translate the following letter of apology:

Dear Mr Rossi,

Thank you for your invitation to the theatre next Tuesday. I am sorry, but unfortunately I cannot come. I am going to Florence on Tuesday and cannot come back until Wednesday.

Please accept my apologies, but I have to go on business and I cannot refuse.

Yours sincerely,

58 EXPRESSIONS USING 'AVERE'

There are many expressions in Italian using **avere** instead of the English verb 'to be':

avere ragione	to be right
avere torto	to be wrong
avere fame	to be hungry
avere sete	to be thirsty
avere freddo	to be cold
avere caldo	to be hot
avere paura	to be afraid
avere fretta	to be in a hurry
avere voglia	to be willing/to feel like

Examples:
Mario ha ragione e tu hai torto.
Mario is right and you are wrong.
Io ho fame e freddo.
I am cold and hungry.

8

To say that you agree or disagree with somebody in Italian you use: **éssere d'accordo/non éssere d'accordo or dare ragione/dare torto**.

Examples:
María ha ragione, ma Antonio le dà sempre torto.
Mary is right, but Antony always disagrees with her.
Sono d'accordo con te.
I agree with you.

Note: **éssere d'accordo con ...** *but* **dare ragione a ...**

Exercise 80

Comment on the statements using the correct expression from the following:

avere fame	avere caldo
avere sete	dare ragione
avere ragione	dare torto
avere torto	avere fretta
avere freddo	avere paura

Example:
Dico che la regina d'Inghilterra si chiama Rita. Io ho torto.

1 Oggi la temperatura è sotto zero. Io ...

2 Non mángiano da due giorni. (loro) ...

3 Mario dice che io sono molto bravo. Io ... !

4 Tutti dícono che María studia poco, ma María ...

5 A Nápoli ci sono 40 gradi. Tutti ...

6 Vogliamo una bottiglia di acqua minerale. (noi) ...

7 Mario pensa sempre di aver ragione, ma io ...

8 Non mi piace viaggiare da sola perchè (io) ...

9 Dévono correre a prendere il treno. (loro) ...

10 Silvia dice che Parigi è in Spagna. Silvia ...

8

60 USE OF THE VERB 'FARE'

Fare is used in many expressions, with different meanings:

1 'to do' and 'to make':

Faccio il tè.	I am making tea.
Che cosa fai?	What do you do?
Faccio fatica.	I make an effort.

2 'to be' with jobs and professions:

Faccio la commessa.
I am a shop assistant.

3 'to take':

Faccio una passeggiata.
I am taking a walk.
Faccio il bagno.
I am taking a bath.

4 'to give':

Ho fatto una conferenza su Dante.
I gave a lecture on Dante.

5 'to get something done':

Faccio riparare la televisione.
I have the TV repaired.
Li faccio studiare.
I make them study.
Mi fa fare tutto!
He makes me do everything!

8

6 to describe the weather:

Fa bel tempo.	The weather is fine.
Fa freddo.	It is cold.

7 in idiomatic expressions:

fare attenzione	to pay attention
far figura/colpo	to impress
fare la coda	to queue
fare il tifo	to support
fárcela	to manage
farla a qualcuno	to trick/deceive somebody
far sapere	to inform, to let [people] know

61 IRREGULAR VERB: 'ACCÓRGERSI'

The verb **accorgersi** (to notice) is irregular in the perfect tense.

	perfect tense	
accórgersi	**mi sono accorto/accorta**	I noticed

8

Exercise 81

Answer the following questions using the correct form of 'fare'.

Examples:

Allora ce l'avete fatta?→ Sì, ce l'abbiamo fatta.
  (Could you manage then?)→ (Yes, we managed.)

Fa l'attrice Lei?→ Sì, faccio l'attrice.
  (Are you an actress?)→ (Yes, I am an actress.)

1 Avete fatto una passeggiata?
2 Ha fatto molte lezioni?
3 Fa brutto tempo oggi?
4 Le fa ripétere l'esercizio?
5 Mi fa vedere quella fotografía?
6 Fate colazione in albergo?
7 Si fa costruire una casa?
8 Vi fa fare molto lavoro?
9 Ce la fa?
10 Avete fatto fatica?

Exercise 82

Translate the following sentences:

1 We decided to go to the exhibition.
2 In my opinion this is the worst film by Fellini.
3 They did not realize that I was very tired.
4 Which is the largest theatre in the world?
5 I don't like music as much as you (fam.) do.
6 Hotels are more expensive in August than in June.
7 Shall we meet in three hours?
8 I am very sorry about being late.
9 Did you enjoy yourself (formal) with your friends yesterday?
10 Did you (formal) manage to find the tickets?

8

Mi dispiace di non éssere venuto.
E il più famoso cantante del mondo.
Non ce la faccio più.
Londra è più grande di Milano.

accettare	to accept
accordo (m.)	agreement
accórgersi	to realize
affettuoso	affectionate, loving
appassionato	fond
assenza (f.)	absence
attore (m.)	actor
attrice (f.)	actress
avér voglia (di)	to feel like, to want
bravo	good, clever
calcio (m.)	football
caldo	hot, warm
cantante (m. & f.)	singer
cattivo	bad
coda (f.)	queue
cómpera (f.)	purchase
conferenza (f.)	lecture
costruire	to build
criticare	to criticize
cúpola (f.)	dome
Egregio	Dear [sir]
davvero	really
dispiacere	to be sorry
distinto	distinguished
Distinti saluti	Yours sincerely/faithfully
disturbo (m.)	bother
duomo (m.)	cathedral
espressivo	intense, with feeling
facilmente	easily
fame (f.)	hunger
fatica (f.)	effort
fárcela	to manage, to cope
fermarsi	to stop, to stay
festa (f.)	party

8

féstival (m.)	festival
Firenze (f.)	Florence
fissare	to arrange
freddo (m.)	cold
fretta (f.)	hurry
gallería (f.)	gallery
genio (m.)	genius
Gentile	Dear [madam]
gentile	kind
grado (m.)	degree
incontrarsi	to meet
insuperábile	unbeatable, outstanding
intelligente	intelligent, clever
inténdere	to understand
interessarsi	to be interested
inverno (m.)	winter
invito (m.)	invitation
lírica (f.)	operatic music, opera
maggiore	greater/older, greatest/oldest
magnífico	magnificent
male	badly
meglio	better (adverb)
migliore	better, best
minore	smaller, smallest/younger, youngest
música (f.)	music
[música] lírica (f.)	operatic music, opera
mondo (m.)	world
mostra (f.)	exhibition
museo (m.)	museum
occasione (f.)	opportunity
palazzo (m.)	palace, block [of flats]
passatempo (m.)	pastime
passeggiata (f.)	walk
passione (f.)	passion, interest
paura (f.)	fear
peggio	worse (adverb)
peggiore	worse
per affari	on business
péssimo	very bad
pregare	to pray, to beg

8

presuntuoso	conceited
ragione (f.)	right, reason
recitare	to act
regata (f.)	regatta
Roma (f.)	Rome
saluto (m.)	greeting
scusare	to forgive, to excuse
senso (m.)	way, sense
sete (f.)	thirst
simpático	likeable
sincero	sincere
sotto	below, under
Spagna (f.)	Spain
spesso	often
spettácolo (m.)	show, spectacle
spettatore (m.)	spectator
storia (f.)	story, history
stórico	historical
straniero	foreign, foreigner
studioso	studious
tanto ... quanto	as much ... as
teatro (m.)	theatre
tecnicamente	technically
tenore (m.)	tenor
tifo (m.) fare il tifo	to support
tifoso	fan, supporter
torto	wrong
trágico	tragic
trovarsi	to meet
turista (m. & f.)	tourist
único	unique
verità (f.)	truth
voce (f.)	voice

8

Week 9

You will learn to:
- describe your job, talk about jobs in general
- choose the appropriate form of address
- discuss current affairs
- spell names, acronyms and e-mail addresses

The grammar will include:
- relative pronouns (who, whom, which, that, etc)
- imperatives of 'fare', 'dire', 'andare'
- da', di', fa', sta', va' with pronouns
- use of gerund (English '-ing' form) and infinitive
- continuous present and imperfect tenses ('sto, stavo + gerund, stare per …')
- negative pronouns and adverbs (nothing, nobody, never, etc)
- irregular verbs: 'eléggere' and verbs ending in '-gliere'

CONVERSATION A

A una riunione di ex-allievi

At an old school reunion Antonio and María meet ten years after leaving school and talk about their jobs.

ANTONIO	**Ciao María, ti ho riconosciuta súbito!**
MARÍA	**Ciao, mi pareva di averti riconosciuto. Sono proprio contenta di rivederti.**
ANTONIO	**Anch'io, sai. E dimmi un po', cosa fai di bello?**
MARÍA	**Faccio l'avvocato, e tu? Ti sei dedicato agli affari, mi pare.**
ANTONIO	**Sì, lavoro per una compagnía che fábbrica computer.**
MARÍA	**Li fai o li vendi?**
ANTONIO	**Li vendo, lavoro nel reparto véndite. È Marco che è diventato un esperto di elettrónica. Ti ricordi di Marco, no?**
MARÍA	**Come no? È lui che mi ha fatto conóscere mio marito!**
ANTONIO	**Davvero? Tuo marito era all'università con lui?**

9

MARÍA   **No, no. Mio marito gestisce un bar, ma vanno spesso in piscina insieme e ci siamo conosciuti lì.**

ANTONIO   **Fammi conóscere tuo marito, e io ti presento la mia compagna. È quella che parla con Tina e Mario. .**

MARÍA   **Beníssimo. Chi è la signora con cui parla Sandro?**

ANTONIO   **Quella è la direttrice della nostra compagnía. Faceva un anno più di noi a scuola.**

TRANSLATION A

At an old school reunion

ANTONIO   Hello María, I recognized you straight away!

MARÍA   Hello, I thought I recognized you. I am really pleased to see you again.

ANTONIO   So am I, you know. Tell me, what do you do now?

MARÍA   I'm a lawyer, and you? You're in business, aren't you?

ANTONIO   Yes, I work for a computer manufacturing company.

MARÍA   Making or selling them?

ANTONIO   I sell them, I work in the sales department. It's Marco who became an expert in electronics. You remember Marco, don't you?

MARÍA   Of course I do! He's the one who introduced me to my husband.

ANTONIO   Really? Was your husband at university with him?

MARÍA   No. My husband runs a bar, but they often go to the swimming pool together and we met there.

ANTONIO   Introduce me to your husband and I'll introduce you to my partner. She is the one talking to Tina and Mario.

MARÍA   Fine. Who is the lady Sandro is talking to?

ANTONIO   She is our company manager. She was in the year above us.

9

62 RELATIVE PRONOUNS: WHO, WHICH, THAT, ETC

The relative pronouns are sometimes omitted in English, but in Italian they are always expressed.

They are:

1 che to translate the English 'who', 'whom', 'which', 'that' when they are not used with a preposition:

la signora che è venuta
the lady who came
gli uómini che hai conosciuto
the men (whom) you met
gli uffici che réstano aperti
the offices that stay open

2 cui used after a preposition and to translate 'whose':

Questa è la ditta per cui lavoro.
This is the firm I work for.
i colleghi con cui lavoro
the colleagues with whom I work
È Marco di cui conosco la moglie.
It is Marco whose wife I know.

3 quello che or **ciò che** when the relative pronoun 'what' in English is used with the meaning of 'that which':

Faccio quello che vuoi.
I'll do what you want.
Ciò che vedi è ciò che ho.
What you see is what I have.
Ti do tutto quello che ho.
I'll give you all I have.

9

4 quelli che (plural) or **chi** (singular) to translate the English 'that/ those/the one/ones/he/she/they/someone who …'

Chi non paga non può venire.
Quelli che non págano non póssono venire.
Those who don't pay can't come.

BUT remember that this is the only time **chi** is used as a relative pronoun. Otherwise it is only used in questions (see Week 2). **Chi** must NEVER be used instead of **che**.

5 il quale (which also takes the forms **la quale, i quali, le quali** and combines with the prepositions **a, di, da, in, su**). It is used almost exclusively in writing and usually for emphasis or to avoid ambiguities:

il padre della signora, del quale ti ho parlato
the lady's husband, about whom I spoke to you
questi colleghi, ai quali non parlo
these colleagues, to whom I don't talk

Exercise 83

Read Conversation A carefully again, then answer these questions using complete sentences:

1 Cosa fa il marito di María?
2 Qual è la compagna di Antonio?
3 Chi è Marco?
4 Che cosa fa Antonio?
5 È Marco che fa l'avvocato?

9

Exercise 84

Complete these sentences using the correct form of the relative pronouns 'che', 'cui', 'quello che', 'quelli che', 'chi', 'il/la quale':

1 Quella signora … parla con María è la mia segretaria.
2 Questa è la Borsa di Milano di … ti ho parlato.
3 Molti degli uffici in … lavoriamo sono al primo piano.
4 Mi dice sempre … vuole.
5 … non stúdiano non pássano gli esami.
6 Lo stipendio … riceviamo è mínimo.
7 Per favore mi potete mandare tutto … avete preparato?
8 La ragazza di Antonio, con … non parlo più, è simpática invece.
9 Questo è l'albergo in … siamo stati durante le vacanze.
10 … non ha visto Roma non conosce l'Italia.

9

Tony is asking Luisa when she uses tu and when she uses Lei.

TONY **Dimmi Luisa, tu a chi dai del tu e a chi del Lei?**

LUISA **Dunque, io do del tu a tutti i gióvani della mia età e naturalmente ai miei parenti, anche a quelli più anziani.**

TONY **E io a chi potrei dare del Lei?**

LUISA **Fa' come me. Da' del tu a tutti eccetto alle persone che non conosci e che sono decisamente più vecchie di te.**

TONY **Per esempio, il giornalaio ti ha dato del tu, ma tu gli hai dato del Lei. Come mai?**

LUISA **Il giornalaio mi conosce da quand'ero bambina, ma io, essendo più gióvane, devo dargli del Lei.**

TONY **Ho capito. Allora io posso dare del tu alla cameriera della mensa che ha più o meno la mia età?**

LUISA **Beh, dipende. Se ti dà del tu, dalle del tu, altrimenti no.**

TONY **Mi pare una cosa un po' delicata!**

LUISA **Sì, è una questione un po' personale. Sta' attento, se non sei sicuro usa il Lei.**

9

TRANSLATION B

TONY Tell me Luisa, who do you use tu with and who do you use Lei with?

LUISA Well, I use tu with all young people of my age and of course with my relatives, even elderly ones.

TONY What about me? Who should I use Lei with?

LUISA Do what I do. Use tu with everybody except people whom you don't know and who are definitely older than you.

TONY For instance, the newsagent used tu with you, but you used Lei with him. Why?

LUISA The newsagent has known me since I was a child, but being younger I must use Lei with him.

TONY I understand. So can I use tu with the canteen waitress who is roughly my age?

LUISA That depends on whether she uses tu with you. If she does, you do the same, otherwise you don't.

TONY It all seems rather tricky!

LUISA Yes, it is quite a personal thing. Be careful and if in doubt use Lei.

Exercise 85

Read Conversation B very carefully, then answer these questions, using a full sentence whenever possible:

1 A chi dà del tu Luisa?
2 Perchè le dà del tu il giornalaio?
3 A chi potrebbe dar del tu Tony?
4 A chi dovrebbe dare del Lei?
5 Luisa dà del Lei a Tony?

9

63 IRREGULAR VERBS: IMPERATIVES OF 'ANDARE', 'DIRE', 'FARE'

	andare	dire	fare
	to go	to say	to do
tu	va'!	di'!	fa'!
Lei	vada!	dica!	faccia!
noi	andiamo!	diciamo!	facciamo!
voi	andate!	dite!	fate!

Examples:

Signora, vada all'ufficio passaporti!
Please go to the passport office, madam!
Fátelo adesso, ragazzi!
Do it now, boys!
Mi dica la verità, signor Rossi!
Mr Rossi, tell me the truth!

64 SHORTENED IMPERATIVES WITH PRONOUNS

When **da'**, **di'**, **fa'**, **sta'** and **va'** – shortened imperative forms – are used with a pronoun, the initial consonant of the pronoun is doubled (except for **gli**):

Dacci oggi il nostro pane quotidiano.
Give us our daily bread.
Dille la verità!
Tell her the truth.
Fammi un favore!
Do me a favour.
Stacci almeno un'ora!
Stay there at least an hour.
Valli a trovare in agosto!
Go and visit them in August.

Note that **ci** means 'there' as well as 'us' and 'to us'. Note also that **andare a trovare** means 'to pay a visit to'.

Exercise 86

Change these imperatives from the 'lei' to the 'tu' form.

Example:
Mi faccia un favore! → Fammi un favore!

1 Mi dia quell'indirizzo!
2 Le faccia vedere l'ufficio!
3 Ci dica la verità!
4 La vada a trovare domani!
5 Mi dia del tu!
6 Ci stia un po' di più!
7 Le faccia il biglietto!
8 Mi dica chi è!
9 Gli faccia una fotografia!
10 Mi dia la mano!

9

CONVERSATION C

Il programma d'attualità

Peter and his landlady are discussing a current affairs
programme they have just watched on television.

PETER **Se ho capito bene l'euro sta salendo
rispetto al dollaro.**

PADRONA **Sì, certo che, considerando il costo della
vita, probabilmente tutto rimane lo stesso.**

PETER **Ma il Presidente del Consiglio ha spiegato
che se gli stipendi non auméntano, anche i
prezzi réstano uguali.**

PADRONA **Mah! I sindacati stanno discutendo proprio
adesso un aumento del sette per cento.**

PETER **Secondo Lei i sindacati avrébbero torto?**

PADRONA **No, ma gli stipendi dovrébbero restare al di
sotto dell 'inflazione .**

PETER **L'inflazione è più bassa in Italia che in
America, vero?**

PADRONA **Sì, al momento sì. Ma ha visto che c'è lo
sciópero dei treni domani?**

PETER **Di tutti i mezzi di trasporto, mi pare. Di
sólito quanto dúrano questi scióperi?**

PADRONA **Lo sciópero generale di sólito dura solo
ventiquattr'ore.**

PETER **Meno male! Perchè vorrei andare via per il
weekend. Ma, a dir la verità, io sono
d'accordo con i ferrovieri.**

PADRONA **Ah si? E perchè?**

PETER **Il loro portavoce ha detto che fanno
sciópero perchè préndono solo in media
uno stipendio di settecento euro al mese.
Non è molto.**

PADRONA **Vedo che Lei è di sinistra. Come mio figlio.
Io sono di destra, invece.**

PETER **In un certo senso sì, in America voto
democrático.**

9

TRANSLATION C

The current affairs programme

PETER   If I understood correctly the euro is going up against the dollar.

LANDLADY   Yes, it is. But if you look at the cost of living, it is all likely to stay the same.

PETER   But the Prime Minister explained that if wages don't go up prices will stay the same too.

LANDLADY   Who knows! The unions are discussing a 7 per cent pay rise at the moment.

PETER   Would you say that the unions are wrong?

LANDLADY   No, I would not, but wages ought to stay below inflation.

PETER   Inflation is lower in Italy than in America, isn't it?

LANDLADY   At the moment it is. But did you see that there is a train strike tomorrow?

PETER   An all-out transport strike, I think. How long are these strikes usually?

LANDLADY   A general strike usually lasts only 24 hours.

PETER   Thank goodness for that! Because I'd like to go away for the weekend. But, quite frankly, I agree with the railmen.

LANDLADY   You do, do you? Why?

PETER   Their spokesman said that they are striking because they get an average of 700 euro a month. That's not much.

LANDLADY   I see that you are left-wing. Like my son. While I am on the right.

PETER   In a way, yes. In America I vote Democrat.

9

Exercise 87

Read Conversation C carefully, check all the new expressions, then try to answer these questions without looking at the text:

1 L'euro sta scendendo?
2 Peter è di destra?
3 Perchè fanno sciópero i ferrovieri?
4 Il costo della vita sta salendo in Italia?
5 Di che cosa stanno parlando Peter e la signora?

65 GERUND ('DOING', 'GOING', ETC)

In Italian the gerund (like the English '-ing' form: 'smoking', 'writing' etc) is formed by removing the ending **-o** from the first person of the present and adding **-ando** (with **-are** verbs) or **-endo** (with **-ere** and **-ire** verbs):

parlare	**vedere**	**uscire**
parlando	**vedendo**	**uscendo**
speaking	seeing	going out

Note that the endings of the gerund are never irregular, but with verbs like **bere**, **dire** etc remember that the stem comes from the first person of the present and not from the infinitive:

bere	**(io bevo)**	**bevendo**
dire	**(io dico)**	**dicendo**
fare	**(io faccio)**	**facendo**

Examples:
Camminando in fretta sono arrivata in cinque minuti.
By walking fast I arrived in 5 minutes.
Uscendo ho visto Paola.
(While I was) going out I saw Paola.

Note that the gerund in Italian must be used without a preposition. When it is necessary to use a preposition, then you must use an infinitive and not a gerund (see section 56).

Note also that in Italian you cannot use a gerund instead of a relative clause or as a noun:

Fumare fa male.
Smoking is harmful.
la ragazza che parla con lui
the girl (who is) talking with him

66 CONTINUOUS PRESENT AND IMPERFECT

If you want to say that you are or were doing something, you sometimes use the continuous present or imperfect tenses in Italian.

These are formed by the present or imperfect of **stare** (not **éssere**) followed by the gerund:

sto mangiando	**stavo mangiando**
I am eating	I was eating

stai	**stavi**
sta	**stava**
stiamo	**stavamo**
state	**stavate**
stanno	**stávano**

But continuous tenses are much less commonly used in Italian than in English. As a general rule you would only need to use them to emphasize what you are doing at a precise moment:

Non può venire adesso, sta mangiando.
He can't come now, he's eating.
Stiamo partendo proprio adesso.
We are leaving this very minute.

9

Stavo uscendo e proprio allora ha suonato il teléfono.
I was going out and just then the phone rang.

Note that object pronouns can be put either before **stare** or at the end of the gerund:

La sto guardando.
or **Sto guardándola.**
I am looking at her.

Exercise 88

Complete the following sentences by adding the gerund of the verbs given in brackets:

1 María e Giovanni stávano (guardare) la partita alla televisione.
2 (studiare) i verbi ho imparato a parlare meglio.
3 (léggere) il giornale seguo le notizie d'attualità.
4 Ho visto il suo vestito (méttere) via la roba.
5 Aspetta, non vedi che l'ascensore sta (venire).
6 Ha fatto i soldi (véndere) frutta e verdura al mercato.
7 Non posso venire al bar, il treno sta (arrivare) proprio adesso.
8 Abbiamo passato la serata (discútere) di política.
9 (fare) colazione al bar arrivo in ufficio presto.
10 Che cosa ti stávano (dire)?

9

67 USE OF 'STARE PER ... '

When you want to say that something is 'about to' or 'going to' happen, in Italian you use **stare per ...** followed by an infinitive:

Fammi sedere! Sto per svenire.
Let me sit down! I am going to faint.
Il treno sta per fermarsi.
The train is about to stop.

68 IRREGULAR VERB: 'ELÉGGERE'

eléggere (to elect)

perfect tense: **ho eletto**

69 NEGATIVE PRONOUNS AND ADVERBS: NOTHING, NOBODY, NEVER, ETC

In Italian all negative pronouns like **niente** (nothing),
nessuno (nobody), **mai** (never), **neanche** (neither, not
even), **nè ... nè** (neither ... nor) etc require **non** before
the verb:

Non conosco nessuno a Roma.
I don't know anybody in Rome.
Non siete mai andati al Vaticano?
Have you never been to the Vatican?
Non mangio nè carne nè pesce.
I eat neither meat nor fish.
Non ci credo neanch'io.
I don't believe it either.

Note that in Italian you can use two or more negatives in
the same sentence:

Non mangia mai niente a colazione.
He never eats anything for breakfast.

BUT if the negative pronoun is used before the verb,
then **non** is not used:

Nessuno ha visitato il castello.
Nobody visited the castle.

9

The 1st person singular and the 3rd person plural of the present of these verbs and the past participle are irregular:

scégliere (to choose)

present tense	perfect tense
scelgo	**ho scelto etc**
scegli	
sceglie	
scegliamo	
scegliete	
scélgono	

	present tense	perfect tense
cógliere (to pick)	**colgo/cólgono**	**colto**
sciógliere (to dissolve)	**sciolgo/sciólgono**	**sciolto**

Exercise 89

Complete these sentences using 'stare per'.
Example:
Non posso chiamarlo: … uscire.→ Sta per uscire.

1 Non posso disturbarli: … uscire.
2 Non posso mandarla a casa: … dormire.
3 Non posso interrómperli: … finire.
4 Non posso invitarlo: … andare in vacanza.
5 Non posso disturbarle: … coricarsi.
6 Non posso portarlo qui a pranzo: … andare al ristorante.
7 Non posso tenerli qui: … partire.
8 Non posso ignorarli: … salutarmi.
9 Non posso telefonarle: … andare a letto.
10 Non posso chiamarli: … préndere l'áutobus.

Exercise 90

Read the following passage carefully and check the words you don't know in the vocabulary at the end of the lesson, then translate it into English.

Lo stato italiano

L'Italia è una repúbblica dal 1946, l'anno in cui c'è stato il referendum per decídere se mantenere la monarchía o no. La monarchía ha perso e la casa di Savoia, che era la casa regnante, è andata in esilio.

La Costituzione, entrata in vigore nel 1948, stabilisce che il Presidente della Repúbblica è Capo dello Stato ma non Capo del Governo; non è eletto dal pópolo ma dai membri del Parlamento.

Il Capo del Governo è il Presidente del Consiglio, che insieme ai Ministri forma il Governo che deve ésser approvato da tutte e due le Cámere.

Il Parlamento consiste della Cámera dei Deputati che ha 630 membri e del Senato che ne ha 315. La Cámera dei Deputati e il Senato sono eletti per cinque anni, il Presidente della Repúbblica per sette anni.

Gli italiani vótano a diciotto anni per la Cámera (dei Deputati), ma póssono votare per il Senato solo all'età di venticinque anni.

9

Exercise 91

Re-translate the passage above into Italian, making
sure that you correct any possible mistakes, then
answer the following questions in full:

1 L'Italia è diventata una Repúbblica nel 1948?

2 Il Presidente della Repúbblica è Capo del Governo?

3 Quanti deputati ci sono alla Cámera?

4 A che età vótano in Italia?

5 Quanti senatori ci sono al Senato?

71 SPELLING, ACRONYMS, AND E-MAIL

ACRONYMS

Most acronyms (like **CIT** or **FIAT**) are read like ordinary
words. But with some, the letters have to be read one
by one:

BBC   **la bi bi ci**

SPELLING

If you want to read less commonly used acronyms, or if
you need to spell your name in Italy, this is how you will
read the letters of the alphabet:

A	**a**	N	**enne**
B	**bi**	O	**o**
C	**cl**	P	**pi**
D	**di**	Q	**qu**
E	**e**	R	**erre**
F	**effe**	S	**esse**
G	**gi**	T	**ti**
H	**acca**	U	**u**
I	**i**	V	**vi**
J	**iota** [i lunga]	W	**doppio vi, vu**
K	**kappa**	X	**ics**
L	**elle**	Y	**ípsilon**
M	**emme**	Z	**zeta**

Note that J, K, W, X and Y are not part of the Italian alphabet.

When spelling out foreign words over the telephone in Italy, you must give each letter followed by the name of a city:

'Root': **'erre' come Roma, 'o' come Otranto, 'o' come Otranto, 't' come Torino.**

READING E-MAIL ADDRESSES

www	**vu vu vu**
@	**chiócciola**
gradi18@libero.it	**gradi diciotto chiócciola libero punto it**

Exercise 92

Translate the following sentences:

1 Give me (fam.) the suitcases, the train is coming in!
2 Not knowing anything, I didn't speak.
3 Not having a passport, I can't leave.
4 He cannot come now because he is eating.
5 Tell me who it is! (fam.)
6 Go there immediately! (fam.)
7 I never choose the seat near the window.
8 It is so hot today, I am going to faint.
9 I cannot invite them, they are about to go out.
10 I did not know the people with whom you (form.) were staying.

9

Non li vada a trovare: stanno per uscire.
Quelli che lavórano con me sono tutti molto bravi.
Dammi del tu!
Mi ha chiamata proprio mentre stavo mangiando.
Non ho mai visto nessuno neanch'io.

alcuni	some, any
al di sotto	below
allievo/a	pupil
altrimenti	otherwise
andare a trovare	to visit, to pay a visit to
anziano	old
approvare	to approve
attento	careful
attualità (f.)	current affairs
aumento (m.)	increase
avvocato (m.)	lawyer
basso	low
Borsa (f.)	Stock Exchange
Cámera (f.)	Chamber
capo (m.)	head, boss
Capo dello Stato (m.)	Head of State
castello (m.)	castle
che	who, whom, that, which
chi	the one/ones who
chiamare	to call
ciò che	what, that which
cógliere	to pick
come mai?	how come?, why?
come no!	yes, certainly! and how!
compagna (f.)	partner, companion
compagnía (f.)	company
comunista	communist
consístere	to consist
cosa (f.)	thing
costo (m.)	cost
cui	whom, which
dare del tu/del lei	to use tu/Lei
dare la mano	to shake hands

9

decisamente	definitely
dedicarsi	to devote oneself
delicato	delicate
democrático	democratic
deputato (m.)	Member of Parliament
dipéndere	to depend
direttrice (f.)	director
discútere	to discuss
disturbare	to bother
diventare	to become
dollaro (m.)	dollar
domani	tomorrow
eccetto	except
eléggere	to elect
elezioni(f. pl.)	elections
elettrónica (f.)	electronics
entrare in vigore	to become law
esilio (m.)	exile
esperto	expert
età (f.)	age
fabbricare	to manufacture
far vedere	to show
ferroviere (m.)	railman
formare	to form
frutta (f.)	fruit
generale	general
gestire	to run (a business)
governo (m.)	government
ignorare	to ignore
il quale	who, whom, which, that
inflazione (f.)	inflation
Inghilterra (f.)	England
interrómpere	to interrupt
invece	instead, on the contrary
invitare	to invite
Italia (f.)	Italy
liberale	liberal
lista (f.)	list
mantenere	to keep
media (f.)	average
membro (m.)	member

9

meno male	thank goodness
mensa (f.)	refectory, canteen
mercato (m.)	market
mezzo (m.)	means
mi pare	I think
momento (m.)	moment
monarchía (f.)	monarchy
notizie (f. pl.)	news
parente (m. & f.)	relative
parlamentare	parliamentary
Parlamento (m.)	Parliament
partita (f.)	match
partito (m.),	party (political party)
per cento	per cent
per esempio	for example
personale	personal
piscina (f.)	swimming pool
pópolo (m.)	people
portavoce (m. & f.)	spokesperson
presentare	to introduce
presidente (m. & f.)	chairperson, president
Presidente del Consiglio	Prime Minister
presto	early
probabilmente	probably
questione (f.)	matter, question
quotidiano	daily
referendum (m.)	referendum
regionale	regional
regione (f.)	region
regnante	ruling
repúbblica (f.)	republic
repubblicano	republican
restare	to stay, to remain
ricévere	to receive
riconóscere	to recognize
ricordarsi	to remember
rivedere	to see again
salire	to climb, to go up
salutare	to greet
scégliere	to choose

9

sciógliere	to dissolve
sciópero (m.)	strike
seguire	to follow
Senato (m.)	Senate
senatore (m.)	senator
sindacato (m.)	trade union
sistema (m.)	system
socialista	socialist
spiegare	to explain
stabilire	to establish, to dictate
stesso	same
stipendio (m.)	salary
suonare	to ring
svéndita (f.)	sale
svenire	to faint
teléfono (m.)	telephone
trasporto (m.)	transport
treno (m.)	train
trovare	to find
ufficio (m.)	office
uguale	same, equal
vacanza (f.)	holiday
vecchio	old
verde	green
vita (f.)	life
votare	to vote
voto (m.)	vote

9

Week 10

You will learn:
- how to engage in small talk
- to talk about yourself, discuss your interests and your job
- to exchange comments on the weather

The grammar will include:
- future tense
- irregular future and conditional tenses
- future perfect and past conditional
- reflexive pronouns 'ci', 'vi', 'si' to translate 'each other'/'one another'
- use of prepositions 'a', 'da', 'di' …
- disjunctive pronouns ('me', 'te', 'lui', 'lei', 'noi', 'voi', 'loro', 'sè')

CONVERSATION A

Una gita in montagna

Tony and Jeff go on a coach trip to Monte Baldo, near Lake Garda. Tony talks to Silvana, a young nurse whom they have just met.

SILVANA	**Scusate, posso sedermi qui con voi?**
TONY	**Certo signorina, si accómodi.**
SILVANA	**Grazie. Siete inglesi, vero?**
TONY	**Sì, siamo di Londra. Il lago ci piace moltíssimo e adesso vorremmo vedere un po' anche i monti vicini.**
SILVANA	**A me la montagna piace anche più del lago. Vedrete che vista stupenda c'è dalla cima!**
TONY	**Non vedo l'ora di arrivare al Monte Baldo! Quanto ci vorrà ancora?**
SILVANA	**Mi hanno detto che arriveremo verso le úndici. E poi dovremo fare una bella camminata di circa due ore.**
TONY	**Noi non siamo abituati alle montagne in Inghilterra. Sarà difficile questa camminata fino alla cima?**
SILVANA	**No, sono sicura di no. Neanch'io sono molto abituata alle camminate. Lavoro a**

Milano tutto l'anno e coi turni che faccio ho poco tempo per gli svaghi!

TONY **Proprio come noi. Lavoriamo in un ospedale e spesso siamo di turno anche al sábato e alla doménica.**

SILVANA **Ma guarda che coincidenza! Io faccio l'infermiera al Policlínico di Milano.**

TONY **Siamo infermieri anche noi ...**

TRANSLATION A

A trip to the mountains

SILVANA Excuse me, may I sit here with you?

TONY Certainly, please do.

SILVANA Thank you. You are English, aren't you?

TONY Yes, we are from London. We like the lake very much and now we would like to see the mountains nearby.

SILVANA I like the mountains even more than the lake. You will see what a marvellous view there is from the top!

TONY I can't wait to get to Monte Baldo! How long will it take?

SILVANA We'll arrive towards 11, they told me. Then we'll have a good two-hour walk.

TONY We are not used to mountains in England. Will it be hard, this walk to the top?

SILVANA No, I am sure it won't. I'm not used to walking either. I work in Milan all year round and, given the hours on duty, I have little leisure time.

TONY It's the same with us. We work in a hospital and we are often on duty even Saturdays and Sundays.

SILVANA What a coincidence! I am a nurse at Milan General Hospital.

TONY We are nurses too ...

10

72 FUTURE TENSE

The future tense is formed in a similar way to the
conditional (see week 5, section 34), by removing the
-e of the infinitive and adding **o, ai, a, emo, ete, anno**
and by changing the **-a** of **-are** into **-e**:

parlare	préndere	finire
parlerò	prenderò	finirò
parlerai	prenderai	finirai
parlerà	prenderà	finirà
parleremo	prenderemo	finiremo
parlerete	prenderete	finirete
parleranno	prenderanno	finiranno

The immediate future in Italian is often expressed by the
present tense, but when you want to talk about a more
distant or unknown future or to express uncertainty you
must use the future tense. Examples:

Véngono domani.
They are coming tomorrow. [I am sure of it.]

But:

Verranno domani.
They will (probably) come tomorrow. [I am not sure.]
Chi vincerà le próssime elezioni?
Who will win the next elections? [We don't know the
outcome.]

10

73 IRREGULAR FUTURE AND CONDITIONAL TENSES

Note that with the future, as with the conditional, a number of verbs have special stems:

1 Some verbs, and their compounds, have a contracted stem:

andare	**andrò**	**andrei**
	I will go	I would go
avere	**avrò**	**avrei**
	I will have	I would have
bere	**berrò**	**berrei**
	I will drink	I would drink
cadere	**cadrò**	**cadrei**
	I will fall	I would fall
dovere	**dovrò**	**dovrei**
	I will have to	I would have to
éssere	**sarò**	**sarei**
	I will be	I would be
potere	**potrò**	**potrei**
	I will be able to	I could
sapere	**saprò**	**saprei**
	I will know	I would know
tenere	**terrò**	**terrei**
	I will keep	I would keep
vedere	**vedrò**	**vedrei**
	I will see	I would see
venire	**verrò**	**verrei**
	I will come	I would come
vívere	**vivrò**	**vivrei**
	I will live	I would live

2 Verbs ending in **-care** and **-gare** insert an **h** following the **-c** and **-g** of the stem (i.e. they keep the hard c and g sounds):

cercare	**cercherò**	**cercherei**
	I will seek	I would seek

pagare	pagherò	pagherei
	I will pay	I would pay

3 Verbs ending in **-ciare**, **-giare**, **-sciare** drop the **i** of the stem:

cominciare	comincerò	comincerei
	I will start	I would start
mangiare	mangerò	mangerei
	I will eat	I would eat
lasciare	lascerò	lascerei
	I will leave	I would leave

4 Some verbs ending in **-are** keep the characteristic vowel of the stem:

dare	darò	darei
	I will give	I would give
fare	farò	farei
	I will do	I would do
stare	starò	starei
	I will stay	I would stay

Exercise 93

Read Conversation A carefully, then answer these questions in full:

1 Dove vanno in gita Jeff, Tony e Silvana?

2 Dovranno camminare molto?

3 A che ora arriveranno al Monte Baldo?

4 Che cosa fa Silvana?

5 Dove lavórano tutti e tre?

10

Exercise 94

Answer these questions using the expression 'prima o poi' (sooner or later) and the future tense.

Example:

Vuole cominciare oggi?→ Prima o poi comincerò.

1 Vuole venire oggi?
2 Vuole pagare oggi?
3 Vuole ballare oggi?
4 Vuole andare oggi?
5 Vuole giocare oggi?
6 Vuole scégliere oggi?
7 Vuole finire oggi?
8 Vuole ordinare oggi?
9 Vuole ritornare oggi?
10 Vuole studiare oggi?

Exercise 95

Change these sentences by adding magari ('perhaps', 'maybe') and the future tense.

Example:

Vado da sola.→ Magari andrò da sola.

I am going alone.→ Perhaps I'll go alone.

1 Véngono a piedi.
2 Possiamo dormire in tenda.
3 Portate voi qualcosa da mangiare.
4 Usciamo più tardi.
5 Fa più bella figura.
6 Non gli danno la mancia.
7 Ci aspéttano all'altra fermata.
8 Canto un'altra aria.
9 Paghi tutto insieme.
10 Gestisce lui il ristorante.

10

74 FUTURE PERFECT AND PAST CONDITIONAL

The future perfect ('I will have done') and the past conditional in Italian are formed with the future or conditional of **avere** and **éssere** plus the past participle of the main verb.

future perfect

avrò	**parlato**	**sarò**	**andato/a**
avrai		**sarai**	
avrà		**sarà**	
avremo		**saremo**	**andati/e**
avrete		**sarete**	
avranno		**saranno**	

past conditional

avrei	**parlato**	**sarei**	**andato/a**
avresti		**saresti**	
avrebbe		**sarebbe**	
avremmo		**saremmo**	**andati/e**
avreste		**sareste**	
avrébbero		**sarébbero**	

Fra due ore saranno arrivati sulla cima.
In two hours they will have got to the top.

Note that the future perfect also expresses probability in the past:

Non hai passato l'esame? Avrai studiato ben poco!
Haven't you passed the exam? You must have studied very little!

The past conditional in Italian is used whenever there is a past tense in the main part of the sentence:

Mi ha detto che sarebbe venuto.
He told me that he would come.

10

CONVERSATION B

Tony and Jeff have made friends with Silvana and are now discussing jobs and interests with her. Tony does all the talking because Jeff cannot speak much Italian yet.

SILVANA	**Da quanto tempo lavorate in ospedale?**
TONY	**Io da tre anni, ma Jeff da due. A me il lavoro piace, e a te?**
SILVANA	**Sì, mi piace, ma è un po' duro. Lavoro quattro o anche cinque turni di dódici ore alla settimana!**
TONY	**Per noi è difficile perchè non abbiamo sempre gli stessi turni e così certe settimane ci vediamo sì e no.**
SILVANA	**Vivete insieme?**
TONY	**Sì, da un anno. Purtroppo noi abbiamo poco tempo per altri interessi. E tu?**
SILVANA	**Mi piace andare a cavallo, ma costa caro a Milano. Mi piace anche andare al cínema.**
TONY	**Io faccio collezione di francobolli, ma a Jeff piácciono cose più artístiche. Va a teatro e al cínema come te.**

TRANSLATION B

SILVANA	How long have you been working at the hospital?
TONY	Three years, but Jeff for two. I like my job, do you?
SILVANA	Yes I do, but it is a little hard. I do four or five twelve-hour shifts per week.
TONY	It is difficult for us because we are not always on duty at the same time, so some weeks we hardly see each other.
SILVANA	Do you live together?
TONY	Yes, we have lived together for a year. Unfortunately we don't have much time for other interests. And you?

10

Exercise 96

Read Conversation B carefully, then answer the
following questions in full:

1 Da quanto tempo lavórano Tony e Jeff in ospedale?

2 Quanti turni fa Silvana alla settimana?

3 Perchè Tony e Jeff si védono sì e no certe
settimane?

4 A Silvana piace andare a cavallo?

5 Che cosa piace a Tony?

75   EACH OTHER/ONE ANOTHER

In Italian you use the reflexive pronouns **ci, vi, si** to
translate 'each other' or 'one another':

Ci conosciamo.
We know each other.
Si parlano.
They speak to one another.
Vi telefonate spesso?
Do you phone each other often?
Si danno del tu.
They use tu with each other.

10

USE OF PREPOSITIONS 'A', 'DA', 'DI'

This is a summary of uses of the prepositions **a**, **da** and **di**, most of which you have already seen.

THE PREPOSITION 'A'
The preposition **a** is used:

1 To translate the English 'to':

Parlo a María.
I speak to Mary.
Vado a Roma.
I go to Rome.

2 To translate the English 'at' or 'in' to indicate place (except with names of countries):

Ábito a Milano.
I live in Milan.
Sto a casa.
I stay at home.

BUT with names of countries you use **in**:

Vivo in Italia.
I live in Italy.

3 To translate the English 'at' with expressions of time:

Arrivo alle due.
I am arriving at two o'clock.
a notte alta
at nightfall

10

4 To express means or manner:

Giochiamo a tennis.
We play tennis.
Vado a piedi.
I am going on foot.
Lavo tutto a mano.
I wash everything by hand.

5 With expressions of distance and price:

Costa tre euro al chilo.
It costs 3 euro a kilo.
Milano è a trecento chilómetri da Venezia.
Milan is 300 km from Venice.

6 With descriptive expressions:

una trota alla griglia
a grilled trout
un vestito a righe
a striped dress

7 With other prepositions such as: **vicino a** (near),
insieme a (together with), **in cima a** (on top of),
davanti a (in front of), **fino a** (as far as), **di fronte a**
(opposite), **in mezzo a** (in the middle of) etc.

THE PREPOSITION 'DA'

The preposition **da** is used:

1 To translate the English 'from':

Il treno parte da Génova.
The train comes from Genoa.
Sono lontano da casa.
I am far from home.

2 To translate the English 'by':

Vivo da sola.
I live by myself.
È curato dal médico.
He is cured by the doctor.

3 To translate the English 'as' in time expressions:

da bambina
as a child
da gióvane
as a young person

4 To translate the English 'for' to express uninterrupted time:

Ábito a Roma da due mesi.
I have lived in Rome for two months.
Studio da tre mesi.
I have been studying for three months.
E morto da un anno.
He has been dead a year.

Note that in these expressions you must use the present tense in Italian.

5 To translate the English 'to' or 'at the house/office/shop of':

Vado dal giornalaio.
I am going to the newsagent's.
Vieni da me?
Are you coming to my place?
Ti fermi da Mario?
Are you staying at Mario's?

10

6 To describe inherent physical characteristics or quality:

una tazza da tè
a tea cup
un francobollo da quaranta centesimi
a 40-cent stamp
È roba da pazzi!
It's sheer lunacy!

7 To express purpose before an infinitive:

Ho molto da fare.
I have a lot to do.
Vorrei qualcosa da léggere.
I'd like something to read.

THE PREPOSITION 'DI'
The preposition **di** is used:

1 To translate the English 'of' or 's (see Week 2):

un albergo pieno di turisti
a hotel full of tourists
la divisa di un infermiere
a nurse's uniform

2 To indicate origin:

Sono di Verona.
I am from [i.e. was born in] Verona.

3 With comparatives (see Week 8):

Il Monte Bianco è più alto del Monte Baldo.
Mont Blanc is higher than Monte Baldo.

10

4 To describe the material of which something is made:

una camicia di cotone
a cotton shirt
una scátola di legno
a wooden box

5 In certain idiomatic expressions:

Mi pare di sì.	I think so.
Dice di no.	He says no.
niente di nuovo	nothing new

6 With other prepositions such as: a **fianco di** (at the side of), **prima di** (before), **a causa di** (because of) etc.

Exercise 97

Complete the following questions with the correct preposition.
Example:
La banca è davanti ... la farmacía.→ La banca è davanti alla farmacía. (The bank is in front of the pharmacy.)

1 Giovanni mi ha detto ... sì.
2 Domani forse andremo ... María.
3 Ho comprato una camicia ... seta.
4 Lavora all'ospedale ... un anno.
5 Silvana è ... Milano.
6 Il giornalaio è di fronte ... la banca.
7 Oggi giochiamo ... calcio.
8 L'áutobus arriva ... le due.
9 Hai molto ... fare?
10 Il suo ufficio è ... duecento metri ... biblioteca.

10

Una gita a Cortina / A trip to Cortina

Peter and Luisa are planning a skiing holiday.

PETER **Hai gli scarponi da sci?**
LUISA **No, pensavo di prénderli a noleggio, con gli sci.**
PETER **Io li ho presi in préstito da Gianni. Ma c'è un negozio che li dà a nolo.**
LUISA **Dov'è? È quello dietro all'ostello?**
PETER **No, è di fianco alla Posta. Ma hai visto che piove?**
LUISA **Allora non possiamo sciare se fa così brutto tempo.**
PETER **Magari a Cortina ci sarà il sole, perchè non ci andiamo lo stesso?**
LUISA **D'accordo, se fa brutto tempo anche lì, ci fermeremo in quel bel ristorante sopra alla funivía.**
PETER **Prendo la mácchina dal garage e ci troviamo di fronte a casa tua.**

TRANSLATION C

PETER Have you got ski boots?
LUISA No, I thought of hiring them, with the skis.
PETER I borrowed them from Gianni. But there is a shop that hires them.
LUISA Where is it? Is it the one behind the hostel?
PETER No, it's next to the post office. But have you noticed that it is raining?
LUISA Then we cannot ski if the weather is so bad.
PETER Perhaps in Cortina it's sunny, why don't we go all the same?
LUISA All right, if the weather is bad there, we can stop at that nice restaurant at the top of the cable car.
PETER I'll get the car from the garage and we'll meet opposite your house.

10

Exercise 98

Read Conversation C very carefully, then answer the following questions in full:

1 Da chi ha preso in préstito gli scarponi Peter?
2 Dove danno sci a nolo?
3 Che tempo fa adesso?
4 Se fa brutto tempo a Cortina cosa faranno?
5 Dove si tróvano Peter e Luisa?

---

77 USE OF DISJUNCTIVE PRONOUNS

These are the disjunctive pronouns in Italian:

me	me
te	you (sing.)
lei	her
Lei	you (formal)
lui	him
noi	us
voi	you (pl.)
loro	them
sè	himself/herself/themselves/oneself

They are used:

1 After a preposition:

Vado con lui.
I am going with him.
Lavora per sè.
He/She works for himself/herself.

2 In exclamations:

Póvera me!	Poor me!
Beati voi!	Lucky you!

10

3 In comparisons:

Sono più vecchio di te.
I am older than you.

4 Instead of direct or indirect object pronouns, for emphasis or when there are two objects:

Parla a me non a voi.
He is speaking to me, not to you.
Carlo chiama me, non te.
Charles is calling me, not you.
A me il teatro non piace.
I (emphatic) don't like the theatre.
Imposterà lui la léttera.
He (emphatic) will post the letter.

10

Exercise 99

Change the words in brackets into the appropriate disjunctive pronouns.

Examples:

Parlo a [María] non a [Enzo].→ Parlo a lei non a lui.

[Mi] teléfona davvero?→ Teléfona davvero a me?

1 [Gli] scriverai davvero?
2 Guardo [il bambino] non [la madre].
3 [Ci] parla, ma non a nessun altro.
4 Siete sicuri che [vi] scriverà?
5 C'è molta gente prima di [Mario].
6 [Le] manderai solo un regalo?
7 Párlano spesso di [Carlo e Marina].
8 Fa tutto da [solo].
9 Andiamo a cavallo con [le ragazze].
10 [Mi] invítano proprio?

Exercise 100

Translate the following sentences:

1 We will write to you (pl.) soon.
2 We have known each other for three years.
3 They bought a silk tie for their father.
4 I work as a nurse in Florence.
5 Do you (fam.) have a lot to do?
6 I want to see you (fam.), not your girlfriend!
7 I will start studying next week.
8 They went to Maria's for supper.
9 Lucky you (form.)!
10 The hospital is opposite the bank.

10

KEY PHRASES & VOCABULARY

Giocheremo a tennis.
Non avranno voluto restare da lei.
Il negozio è dietro alla banca.
Forse domani farà bel tempo.

VOCABULARY

a causa di	because of
a fianco di	at the side of, next to
aiuto (m.)	help
alto	high, tall
aria (f.)	air, tune
artístico	artistic
assegno (m.)	cheque
beato	lucky (in exclamations), blessed
biblioteca (f.)	library
blusa (f.)	blouse
camminata (f.)	walk
cantare	to sing
cavallo (m.)	horse
cercare	to look for
chilómetro (m.)	kilometre
cínema (m.)	cinema
circa	about, approximately
coincidenza (f.)	coincidence
collezione (f.)	collection
cotone (m.)	cotton
curare	to cure
dietro a	behind
di fronte a	opposite
di turno	on duty
divisa (f.)	uniform
duro	hard
éssere abituato a	to be used to
fare bella figura	to look good, to impress
fare conoscenza	getting acquainted
farmacía (f.)	pharmacy
fermata (f.)	stop
fino a	as far as
francobollo (m.)	stamp

funivía (f.)	cable car
gente (f.)	people
gita (f.)	trip
guida (f.)	guide
in cima a	on top of
infermiere/a	nurse
insieme a	together with
legno (m.)	wood
lì	there
magari	perhaps, maybe
médico (m.)	doctor
montagna (f.)	mountain
monte (m.)	mount, mountain
morire	to die
morto	dead
noleggio, nolo (m.)	hire
non vedér l'ora di	to look forward to
ordinare	to order
pazzo	mad
piedi (m. pl.)	feet
Policlínico	General Hospital
posta (f.)	mail/post office
póvero	poor
préndere in préstito	to borrow
prestare	to lend
préstito (m.)	loan
prima di	before
riga (f.)	stripe, line
scarponi (m. pl.)	boots
scátola (f.)	box
sci (m. pl.)	skis
sciare	to ski
seta (f.)	silk
sì e no	hardly
svago (m.)	pastime
turno (m.)	duty, shift
ufficio postale (m.)	post office

10

Key to exercises

In this key we have printed only the accents that are normally printed in modern Italian. We have not printed the acute accents which are included in the rest of the course to show you where words are stressed. Remember that these are not normally printed in Italian and you should not get into the habit of writing them yourself.

Week I

Exercise 1: 1 Si, è americana. 2 No, è italiano. 3 Sì, è libera. 4 Sì, è americano. 5 Sì, è solo per oggi. 6 Sì, è italiana. 7 No, è americana. 8 Si, è italiano. 9 Si, è singola. 10 No, è singola.

Exercise 2: 1 Non sono di Verona. 2 Sandro Bianchi non ha una bella casa. 3 L'albergo non è pieno. 4 La signorina non lavora in un albergo. 5 Non parlate bene l'italiano?

Exercise 3: 1 Questo è lo Zoo. 2 Parliamo bene l'italiano. 3 Il marito di Mary è inglese. 4 Rita è la moglie di Sandro. 5 Ascolto l'opera alla Scala. 6 La signora è italiana. 7 L'albergo è molto comodo. 8 Questa è la camera singola. 9 Ecco la chiave. 10 Ecco il passaporto.

Exercise 4: 1 No, è americano. 2 Si chiama Mary. 3 Abita a Venezia. 4 Sono di Milano. 5 Sandro lavora a Venezia. 6 Sì, lavora in un albergo. 7 Sì, è una commessa. 8 No, lavora a New York City. 9 Mary è insegnante. 10 Sì, Mary e John abitano in una casa con giardino.

Exercise 5: 1 Abito a Milano. 2 Lavora a Venezia? 3 Dove abita? 4 Sono una commessa. 5 Rita Rossi parla italiano. 6 Abitiamo a Pavia e lavoriamo a Milano. 7 New York City è bella. 8 Avete il passaporto americano? 9 Di dove siete? 10 Sono americano/a.

Week 2

Exercise 6: 1 No, è un po' piccola. 2 È in fondo al corridoio a destra. 3 Sì. 4 Nello sgabuzzino. 5 È vicino alla cucina.

Exercise 7: 1 Queste sono le mie camere. 2 I bagni sono occupati. 3 Lavoriamo per la nostra compagnia. 4 Gli studenti americani studiano molto. 5 Le sue valigie sono vuote. 6 I pasti cominciano dopo le nove. 7 I nostri pensionanti parlano bene le lingue. 8 Le signore arrivano con le figlie. 9 Se le porte sono aperte noi entriamo. 10 Gli appartamenti al primo piano sono spaziosi.

Exercise 8: 1 Ha tre camere da letto. 2 È al quarto piano. 3 Va a casa di María. 4 No, vive in periferia. 5 Sì, c'è la metropolitana vicino.

Exercise 9:
... abito in periferia.
... c'è la metropolitana vicino.
... una casa piccola con un giardino grande.
... una cucina grande.
... due camere da letto e un bagno.
... è abbastanza vicino.

Exercise 10: 1 vive 2 dormono 3 prendiamo 4 sentite 5 apri 6 vedete 7 vestono 8 sentite 9 mette 10 conosciamo

Exercise 11: 1 i suoi 2 Il suo 3 la loro 4 i vostri 5 i miei 6 tua 7 la nostra 8 mio 9 le Sue 10 le vostre

Exercise 12: 1 Sì, ha bambini. 2 No. L'affitto del garage è extra. 3 No. Non desidera avere la biancheria. 4 È in Piazza Indipendenza. 5 Sì, c'è tutto il necessario.

Exercise 13: 1 È del signor Rossi. 2 È degli studenti. 3 È del mio amico. 4 È della signora Rossi. 5 È dei bambini.

Exercise 14: 1 allo 2 al 3 alla 4 ai 5 alle 6 all' 7 agli

Exercise 15: 1 Troviamo gli appartamenti ammobiliati sui giornali. 2 Le figlie delle signore vivono con i loro ragazzi. 3 Non vediamo la differenza tra queste case e le altre. 4 Le chiavi delle porte sono dalle portinaie. 5 Gli inquilini prendono le cartoline dalle cassette delle lettere.

Exercise 16: 1 Metto la mia macchina in garage. 2 Parto per l'ufficio da solo. 3 Scrivi a tua sorella oggi?/Scrive a Sua sorella oggi? 4 Suo fratello vive qui? 5 Sente molto rumore nella strada affollata.

Exercise 17: 1 María vive con suo padre a Roma. 2 Il mio appartamento è vicino al centro di Milano. 3 Di chi è questa camera? È dei bambini. 4 La loro cucina è piccola. 5 Dove abitate, in un appartamento o in una casa?

Week 3

Exercise 18: 1 Va alla CIT. 2 Desidera una cartina di Roma. 3 Dal tabaccaio o dal giornalaio. 4 Per settantacinque minuti.

Exercise 19: 1 Quella cartina è gratis. 2 Quell'autobus è affollato. 3 Quel treno è veloce. 4 Quello scompartimento è riservato. 5 Partite con quegli amici di Emma? 6 Porti quelle valigie in stazione? 7 Quei biglietti sono di andata e ritorno. 8 Quegli orari non sono giusti. 9 Parti con quell'aereo? 10 Sono liberi quei posti?

Exercise 20: 1 Questo è il mio posto. 2 Questi biglietti sono validi per tre ore. 3 Questi sono i miei ospiti italiani. 4 Prendiamo quel treno. 5 È quella la fermata? 6 Quei bambini sono inglesi. 7 Viaggiamo su quell'autobus. 8 Quelle sono le mie valigie. 9 Quello sportello è aperto. 10 Questa è la stazione.

Exercise 21: 1 Va in Piazza Navona. 2 Sono le undici e mezzo. 3 A mezzogiorno. 4 Ci vuole circa un quarto d'ora. 5 Il venticinque.

Exercise 22: 1 Sono le due e mezzo. 2 Sono le tre. 3 Sono le ventuno. 4 Sono le dodici e quindici/È mezzogiorno e un quarto. 5 È mezzanotte/ Sono le ventiquattro. 6 Sono le quattro e tre quarti/Sono le cinque meno un quarto. 7 Sono le otto e trentacinque. 8 È l'una e mezzo. 9 Sono le due e cinquanta/Sono le tre meno dieci. 10 Sono le sette e dieci.

Exercise 23: 1 A che ora parte l'autobus? Alle sei. 2 A che ora parte l'aereo? Alle sette e trenta. 3 A che ora parte il treno? Alle ventidue e trenta. 4 A che ora arriva il treno? Alle diciassette e venticinque. 5 A che ora arriva l'autobus? Alle tredici e quindici.

Exercise 24: 1 È andato alla stazione. 2 Perchè il treno è partito in ritardo. 3 È partita da Siena. 4 Ha prenotato il ristorante. 5 Ha preparato la camera per Luisa.

Exercise 25: 1 Ieri Mario è arrivato alle tre. 2 Ieri il treno è partito alle nove. 3 Ieri l'autobus è arrivato in ritardo. 4 Ieri Maria è partita con il treno. 5 Ieri i signori Bianchi sono arrivati alle due. 6 Ieri le valigie sono cadute per terra. 7 Ieri la signorina è andata in macchina. 8 Ieri noi siamo partite all'una. 9 Ieri voi siete andati in treno? 10 Ieri i viaggiatori sono andati a prendere il taxi.

Exercise 26: 1 Un'ora fa ho guidato la macchina. 2 Un'ora fa ho mangiato il pranzo. 3 Un'ora fa María ha preparato la colazione. 4 Un'ora fa abbiamo venduto la nostra macchina. 5 Un'ora fa hanno comprato i biglietti. 6 Un'ora fa i passeggeri hanno guardato l'orario. 7 Un'ora fa hai sentito questo rumore? 8 Un'ora fa abbiamo finito il pranzo. 9 Un'ora fa abbiamo prenotato il ristorante. 10 Un'ora fa hanno portato le valigie sul treno.

Exercise 27:
– Beníssimo, grazie. Ma l'aereo è partito in ritardo da Roma. Così sono arrivato a Cagliari in ritardo.
– Alle dieci e tre quarti, ma sono partito da casa alle sette.
– No, ho preso una macchina a noleggio.
– Sì, ma ho deciso di prendere la macchina a noleggio per una settimana.
– Non ho visto il centro. Vorrei andare in tutti i posti famosi.

Exercise 28: Oggi Francesca è tornata dalla Sardegna. È arrivata in aereo, l'aereo ha fatto scalo ad Alghero e il volo è durato tre ore. È stata a Cagliari poi ha preso una macchina a noleggio ed è andata a Nuoro per due giorni, ma non ha avuto molto tempo per vedere la città. Ha firmato il contratto per il nuovo albergo. Ha visto anche il nuovo direttore. Ha fatto molto, ma la prossima volta desidera restare più a lungo.

Week 4

Exercise 29: 1 Rita vuole affittare un appartamento. 2 Non posso guardare questa lista? 3 Vorrei prenotare una camera. 4 Non possiamo pagare molto. 5 Dobbiamo partire alle nove. 6 Volete andare al campeggio? 7 Possono venire oggi. 8 Deve pagare di più. 9 Vuole stare in una pensione? 10 Se posso voglio stare a Venezia per tre giorni.

Exercise 30: 1 Devo andare più tardi. 2 Devo aspettare alla stazione. 3 Devo vedere la mia padrona di casa. 4 Voglio venire alle tre. 5 Voglio restare all'albergo. 6 Voglio vedere i miei amici. 7 Posso venire a mezzogiorno. 8 Posso restare al campeggio. 9 Posso invitare una collega. 10 Posso pagare stasera.

Exercise 31: 1 Vuole una casetta in campagna. 2 Preferisce abitare in campagna. 3 Sì, può trovare un appartamento non restaurato. 4 Sì, ma deve telefonare al mattino. 5 Sì, c'è l'acqua.

Exercise 32: 1 Sì, scriva pure! 2 Sì, cominci pure! 3 Sì, finisca pure! 4 Sì, mangi pure! 5 Sì, pulisca pure! 6 Sì, chiuda pure! 7 Sì, serva pure! 8 Sì, guardi pure! 9 Sì, parta pure! 10 Sì, entri pure!

Exercise 33: 1 Sì, scrivi pure! 2 Sì, comincia pure! 3 Sì, finisci pure! 4 Sì, mangia pure! 5 Sì, pulisci pure! 6 Sì, chiudi pure! 7 Sì, servi pure! 8 Sì, guarda pure! 9 Sì, parti pure! 10 Sì, entra pure!

Exercise 34: 1 Scusate, dobbiamo scrivere? Sì, scrivete pure! 2 Scusate, dobbiamo cominciare? Sì, cominciate pure! 3 Scusate, dobbiamo finire? Sì, finite pure! 4 Scusate, dobbiamo mangiare? Sì, mangiate pure! 5 Scusate, dobbiamo pulire? Sì, pulite pure! 6 Scusate, dobbiamo

chiudere? Sì, chiudete pure! 7 Scusate, dobbiamo servire?
Sì, servite pure! 8 Scusate, dobbiamo guardare? Sì, guardate
pure! 9 Scusate, dobbiamo partire? Sì, partite pure!
10 Scusate, dobbiamo entrare? Sì, entrate pure!

Exercise 35: 1 Signorina, non chiuda la finestra, per favore!
2 Mario, non portare la mia valigia, per favore! 3 Piero non
guardare la televisione, per favore! 4 Signorina, non prenda
la chiave, per favore! 5 María, non prendere la chiave, per
favore! 6 Ragazzi, non guardate questo salotto, per favore!
7 Ragazze, non prendete questa strada, per favore! 8 Signor
Rossi, non guardi là per favore. 9 Non scendiamo insieme le
scale! 10 Sandro, non prendere l'ombrello!

Exercise 36: 1 Sì, certo, vada pure! 2 Sì, certo, stia pure!
3 Sì, certo, faccia pure! 4 Sì, certo, dia pure! 5 Sì, certo,
tenga pure! 6 Sì, certo, venga pure! 7 Sì, certo, finisca pure!
8 Sì, certo, pulisca pure! 9 Sì, certo, beva pure! 10 Sì, certo,
legga pure!

Exercise 37: 1 Oggi è martedì. 2 È il trentun gennaio
duemila e due. 3 Costa centomila euro. 4 Costa
ottanta-cinquemila euro. 5 Costano trenta centesimi.
6 Ha trecentomila abitanti. 7 È finita nel
millenovecentoquaranta-cinque. 8 È nata nel
millenovecentotrentadue. 9 Costa sei euro e sessantacinque
(centesimi). 10 Costa centoventi euro.

Exercise 38: 1 Ci sono le docce, i gabinetti, la cucina e la
lavanderia. 2 No, hanno la roulotte. 3 No, non hanno
prenotato il posto. 4 Sì, c'è un supermercato al campeggio.

Exercise 39: 1 Devono prenotare la stanza prima di agosto.
2 Non sono andati in Italia nel millenovecentoottantanove.
3 Preferiamo un appartamento al pianterreno. 4 Vogliono
comprare una casa in campagna. 5 Possiamo guardare il
rustico la settimana prossima? 6 L'appuntamento è per
venerdì prossimo alle quindici. 7 L'agenzia immobiliare può
fissare una visita al mattino. 8 Vorrei venire, ma oggi devo
stare a casa. 9 Mi dispiace, ma vorrei una camera con bagno.
10 Non compri questa casa, è troppo lontano dal centro.

Week 5

Exercise 40: 1 No, non lo prende. 2 Lo offre la signora Fazzini. 3 La offre il signor White. 4 Sì, lo prende. 5 Sì, le mangiano.

Exercise 41: 1 Sì, la guardo spesso. 2 Sì, le compro spesso. 3 Sì, li invito spesso. 4 Sì, lo bevo spesso. 5 Sì, lo prendo spesso. 6 Sì, la porto spesso. 7 Sì, le mangio spesso. 8 Sì, li bevo spesso. 9 Sì, li bevo spesso. 10 Sì, la invito [l'invito] spesso.

Exercise 42: 1 Le parlo adesso. 2 Gli parlo adesso. 3 Gli telefono adesso. 4 Le rispondo adesso. 5 Gli scrivo [scrivo loro] adesso. 6 Gli scrivo [scrivo loro] adesso. 7 Gli rispondo [rispondo loro] adesso. 8 Gli telefono adesso. 9 Gli parlo [parlo loro] adesso. 10 Le scrivo adesso.

Exercise 43: 1 Le dà il numero. 2 Non lo sento. 3 Il signor Forti la legge. 4 La signora le prende. 5 Li compriamo qui. 6 Gli offro [offro loro] l'aperitivo. 7 Gli telefono. 8 Le scrivete? 9 Che cosa gli portate? 10 Il signor Rossi non la lascia.

Exercise 44: 1 Beve un caffè corretto. 2 No, beve un caffè corretto. 3 È un posto dove si beve soprattutto il vino. 4 Tony offre da bere. 5 Lo beve Jeff.

Exercise 45: 1 Sì, dovremmo partire ma abbiamo cambiato idea. 2 Sì, dovrei andare ma non ho la macchina. 3 Sì, potrei venire ma più tardi. 4 Sì, potremmo accompagnarlo in macchina. 5 Sì, vorrei telefonare ma non ho la moneta. 6 Sì, vorremmo viaggiare ma non da soli. 7 No, vorrei un cappuccino. 8 No, vorremmo mangiare alle due. 9 No, potrei venire in bicicletta. 10 Sì, dovremmo restare per la cena.

Exercise 46: 1 Sì, lo compri! 2 Sì, la mangi! 3 Sì, le parli! 4 Sì, li venda! 5 Sì, le prenoti! 6 Sì, la faccia! 7 Sì, la dia! 8 Sì, li porti! 9 Sì, gli telefoni! 10 Sì, lo prenda!

Exercise 47: 1 Sì, compralo! No, non comprarlo! 2 Sì, mangiala! No, non mangiarla! 3 Sì, parlale ! No, non parlarle! 4 Sì, vendili! No, non venderli! 5 Sì, prenotale! No, non prenotarle! 6 Sì, falla! No, non farla! 7 Sì, dalla! No, non darla! 8 Sì, portali! No, non portarli! 9 Sì, telefonagli! No, non telefonargli! 10 Sì, prendilo! No, non prenderlo!

Exercise 48: 1 può 2 so 3 sai 4 so 5 possiamo 6 sa 7 sa 8 posso 9 possono 10 sa

Exercise 49: 1 Sì, mi piace moltissimo. 2 Sì, mi piacciono moltissimo. 3 Sì, mi piace moltissimo. 4 Sì, mi piace moltissimo. 5 Sì, mi piacciono moltissimo. 6 No, non mi piacciono. 7 No, non mi piace. 8 No, non mi piacciono. 9 No, non mi piace. 10 No, non mi piacciono.

Exercise 50: 1 L'amico di Luigi, perchè è vegetariano. 2 Ci sono l'insalata, le patate fritte, i finocchi, verdure fresche. 3 No, li prende solo la signora. 4 No, lo ordina rosso. 5 No, c'è anche trota. 6 Tre persone la mangiano.

Exercise 51: 1 Non ci piace viaggiare in treno. 2 Le piacciono le patate fritte? 3 Per favore dia questa chiave alla signora Rossi. 4 Andresti da solo? 5 María, non prendere la mia macchina, prendi la tua. 6 Gli abbiamo dato tutte le informazioni necessarie. 7 Vi posso offrire qualcosa da bere? 8 Da quanto [tempo] studiate l'italiano? 9 Comprerebbero l'appartamento, ma costa centomila euro. 10 Siamo andati a pranzo da Tony.

Week 6

Exercise 52: 1 La fa dal droghiere. 2 Ne compra più di due etti. 3 Preferisce il reggiano. 4 Ne compra due.

Exercise 53: 1 Ne vorrei un litro. 2 Ne vorrei un chilo e mezzo. 3 Ne vorrei una sola. 4 Ne vorrei due etti. 5 Ne vorrei due chili. 6 Ne ho una. 7 Ne ho quattro. 8 Non ne ho molte. 9 Ne ho pochi. 10 Non ne ho.

Exercise 54: 1 Sì, li ho invitati. 2 Sì, l'ho visitata. 3 Sì l'ho visitato. 4 Sì, li ho portati. 5 Sì, le ho mangiate. 6 Sì, l'abbiamo invitata. 7 Sì, l'abbiamo guardato. 8 Sì, le abbiamo comprate. 9 Sì, l'abbiamo presa. 10 Sì, l'abbiamo visto.

Exercise 55: 1 Vuole il quarantasei. 2 Lo preferisce blù. 3 Sono al terzo piano. 4 Porta il quarantadue. 5 Li compra per gli amici americani.

Exercise 56: 1 Sì, glieli porto. 2 Sì, gliela scrivo. 3 Sì, glielo do. 4 Sì, glieli do. 5 Sì, glielo porto. 6 Sì, gliele scrivo. 7 Sì, gliela compro. 8 Sì, glieli compro. 9 Sì, glielo vendo. 10 Sì, gliela vendo.

Exercise 57: 1 Ha portato i panini ai ragazzi? Sì, glieli ho portati. 2 Ha scritto la lettera a María? Sì, gliel'ho scritta. 3 Ha dato il conto alla signora? Sì, gliel'ho dato. 4 Ha dato i soldi alla signora? Sì, glieli ho dati. 5 Ha portato il vestito al signor Bianchi? Sì, gliel'ho portato. 6 Ha scritto le lettere a tutti? Sì, gliele ho scritte. 7 Ha comprato la pasta per gli ospiti? Si, gliel'ho comprata. 8 Ha comprato i grissini per María? Si, glieli ho comprati. 9 Ha venduto l'appartamento a questi signori? Si, gliel'ho venduto. 10 Ha venduto la casa a questi signori? Sì, gliel'ho venduta.

Exercise 58: 1 Me l'ha consigliato un'amica. 2 Me l'ha dato il poliziotto. 3 Me l'ha portata il facchino. 4 Me l'ha riparato l'orologiaio. 5 Me li ha mandati un amico. 6 Ce l'ha portato il cameriere. 7 Ce le ha vendute la commessa. 8 Ce li ha comprati nostra figlia. 9 Ce l'ha prenotato l'agenzia. 10 Ce l'ha data l'impiegata.

Exercise 59a: 1 Sì, me lo porti pure. 2 Sì, me li mandi pure. 3 Sì, me le regali pure. 4 Sì, me la scriva pure. 5 Sì, me lo prenoti pure.

Exercise 59b: 1 Sì, preparamela pure! 2 Sì, mandamele pure! 3 Sì, comprameli pure! 4 Sì, scrivimelo pure! 5 Sì, prendimela pure!

Exercise 60: 1 Il reparto calzature è al decimo piano. 2 Questa è la sesta settimana. 3 Il primo maggio è una festa nazionale in Italia. 4 Viviamo nel ventunesimo secolo. 5 Prenda la quarta via alla Sua sinistra.

Exercise 61: 1 L'ha messa dentro il Bancomat. 2 C'è scritto che ha aspettato troppo. 3 Sì, è chiusa. 4 No, non li ha persi. 5 Perchè non è riuscito a ritirare i soldi dal Bancomat.

Exercise 62: Ieri Tony e Luisa sono andati alla Rinascente per comprare due regali: uno per la madre di Tony e l'altro per quella di Luisa. Luisa è andata al pianterreno, al reparto accessori, e ha comprato una borsetta di pelle. Tony è andato a dare un'occhiata al reparto casalinghi al sesto piano. Ha guardato i servizi da tè e da caffè, ma non li ha comprati.

Alle quattro Tony e Luisa sono andati a prendere il tè a un bar in Piazza del Duomo e Luisa gli ha fatto vedere la borsetta. Dopo due ore hanno deciso di tornare alla Rinascente perchè Luisa ha visto che la cerniera della borsetta è rotta. L'ha portata indietro all'Ufficio Reclami e ha chiesto un rimborso dei soldi o un'altra borsetta. L'impiegato le ha domandato la ricevuta e dopo molte difficoltà le ha dato una borsetta nuova. Tony nel frattempo ha guardato dappertutto, ma non ha trovato niente per la madre di Luisa. Questo non è stato un pomeriggio molto fortunato per i due giovani!

Week 7

Exercise 63: 1 Perchè ha mal di stomaco. 2 Sì, si preoccupa molto. 3 La deve prendere tre volte al giorno. 4 Deve tornare tra una settimana. 5 No, ha una forma leggera di gastroenterite.

Exercise 64: 1 Mi alzo alle otto. 2 Mi corico alle undici. 3 Mi lavo tutte le mattine. 4 Mi stanco a lavorare troppo. 5 Non mi arrabbio mai. 6 Mi annoio a far la coda. 7 Mi diverto in vacanza. 8 Mi sveglio alle sette e mezzo. 9 Mi riposo dopo pranzo. 10 Mi perdo se non ho la cartina.

Exercise 65: 1 Quando cado mi faccio male. 2 Quando sono andati a letto si sono addormentati. 3 Ieri è andata dal dottore perchè si è sentita male. 4 María è stata a letto quando si è ammalata. 5 Abbiamo fatto il bagno, poi ci siamo asciugati. 6 Non ti ho telefonato perchè mi sono dimenticato/a. 7 María e Giovanni sono andati in chiesa e si sono sposati. 8 Non prendo più le medicine perchè mi sento bene. 9 Quando sono sporchi si lavano. 10 Se scrivo la lista della spesa, mi ricordo.

Exercise 66: 1 Perchè c'è stato un incidente. 2 È stato investito da un motorino. 3 Perchè si è messo a correre per prendere l'autobus. 4 L'hanno portato al Pronto Soccorso. 5 Peter era alla fermata dell'autobus.

Exercise 67: 1 Sì, studiavo quando ero piccolo. 2 Sì, facevo molti sport quando ero a scuola. 3 Sì, viaggiavo molto quando abitavo in Italia. 4 Sì, andavo sempre in macchina quando lavoravo in centro. 5 Sì, sentivo molto i rumori quando dormivo al pianterreno. 6 Sì, facevamo molte gite quando eravamo in montagna. 7 Sì, andavamo fuori spesso quando abitavamo a Milano. 8 Sì, fumavamo quando avevamo diciotto anni. 9 Sì, mangiavamo solo verdura quando vivevamo in Inghilterra. 10 Sì, compravamo sempre il giornale quando lavoravamo in Italia.

Exercise 68: 1 Perchè ero malato. 2 Perchè ero indisposto. 3 Perchè ero arrabbiato. 4 Perchè ero troppo stanco. 5 Perchè ero distratto. 6 Perchè eravamo senza soldi. 7 Perchè eravamo malati. 8 Perchè eravamo stanchi. 9 Perchè eravamo in ritardo. 10 Perchè eravamo molto preoccupati.

Exercise 69: 1 Una volta viaggiavate molto. 2 Una volta ci preoccupavamo molto. 3 Una volta viaggiavano molto. 4 Una volta scrivevi molto. 5 Una volta lavorava molto. 6 Una volta mi divertivo molto. 7 Una volta uscivamo molto. 8 Una volta fumavo molto. 9 Una volta leggevi molto. 10 Una volta parlavano molto.

Exercise 70: 1 Ieri ho preso l'autobus perchè ero stanca. 2 Ieri non ho guardato la televisione perchè non funzionava. 3 Ieri ero a Firenze e sono andata agli Uffizi. 4 Ieri siamo andati dal dottore perchè avevamo la febbre. 5 Ieri il dottore ti ha visitata in casa quando eri a letto malata. 6 Ieri sono alzata alle dieci perchè era festa. 7 Ieri mentre leggevo il giornale è entrato il mio ospite. 8 Ieri mentre scrivevo la lettera i bambini hanno mangiato tutti i cioccolatini. 9 Ieri Sandra aveva mal di testa e non è andata a lavorare. 10 Ieri mentre camminavo lungo la strada ho visto un incidente.

Exercise 71: 1 Perchè ha preso [si è preso] una scottatura al viso. 2 Gli prescrive una pomata. 3 Non solo sul viso ma anche sulla schiena e sulle gambe. 4 Finchè l'arrossamento non è passato. 5 Se si spella deve mettere un'altra pomata protettiva.

Exercise 72:
– Ho mal di schiena.
– Da due giorni.
– Sì, mi fa molto male. È una cosa seria?
– Che cos'è uno strappo muscolare? Cosa devo fare?
– Può darmi qualcosa per dormire?
– Grazie dottore!

Exercise 73: 1 aveva risposto 2 erano andati 3 eravate stati 4 aveva scritto 5 non aveva mai rotto 6 si era fatto male 7 era successo 8 avevo messo 9 aveva chiuso 10 ci eravamo già seduti

Week 8

Exercise 74: 1 No, secondo lei, Domingo ha una voce più calda ed espressiva. 2 Perchè, secondo lui, Pavarotti è il miglior tenore del mondo. 3 Tecnicamente, Pavarotti canta meglio. 4 Sì, le è piaciuto. 5 No, non si interessa di sport. 6 Fa il tifo per l'Inter.

Exercise 75: 1 Ci sono più di trentamila spettatori all'Arena. 2 Secondo me, Roma è più grande di Milano. 3 Giovanni è più studioso che intelligente. 4 Ci sono più teatri a Roma che a Torino. 5 Conosco più attori italiani che stranieri. 6 Sua figlia è più alta di lei. 7 Fa più caldo in Italia che in Inghilterra. 8 Parla più piano di me. 9 Luisa mangia più di tutti. 10 L'Aida mi piace più di Rigoletto.

Exercise 76: 1 Questo è il peggior vino del mondo!
2 Siamo bravi come voi in italiano. 3 C'erano più di ventim-
ila spettatori. 4 María Callas era una cantante famosissima
[molto famosa]. 5 San Paolo non è grande come San Pietro.
6 Giovanni beve più vino che acqua. 7 Mi sento meglio
adesso. 8 Questi programmi sono noiosissimi [molto noiosi].
9 Non abbiamo comprato tanti regali quanto [quanti] voi.
10 Mia sorella minore vive a Milano.

Exercise 77: 1 Vuole vedere la mostra. 2 Perchè vuole
andare alla Chiesa del Carmine. 3 Si trovano davanti
all'Accademia. 4 Hanno comprato dei regali per i loro amici.
5 Vanno in una trattoria.

Exercise 78: 1 hanno deciso di 2 Cominciamo a 3 Spera di
4 Non mi piace 5 Le piace 6 Preferisce 7 devono
8 Ho finito di 9 Credono [Pensano] di 10 Andiamo a

Exercise 79:
Caro Signor Rossi,
    La ringrazio del Suo invito a teatro per martedì prossimo.
Mi dispiace, ma purtroppo non posso venire. Vado a Firenze
martedì e non posso tornare fino a mercoledì.
    La prego di accettare le mie scuse, ma devo andare per
affari e non posso rifiutare.
    Distinti saluti,

Exercise 80: 1 Io ho freddo. 2 Hanno fame. 3 Io gli do
ragione! 4 ma María gli dà torto. 5 Tutti hanno caldo.
6 Abbiamo sete. 7 ma io gli do torto. 8 perchè ho paura.
9 Hanno fretta. 10 Silvia ha torto.

Exercise 81: 1 Sì, l'abbiamo fatta. 2 Sì, ne ho fatte molte.
3 Sì, fa brutto tempo. 4 Sì, me lo fa ripetere. 5 Sì, gliela
faccio vedere. 6 Sì, la facciamo in albergo. 7 Sì, me la faccio
costruire. 8 Sì, ci fa fare molto lavoro. 9 Sì, ce la faccio.
10 Sì, abbiamo fatto fatica.

Exercise 82: 1 Abbiamo deciso di andare alla mostra.
2 Secondo me, questo è il peggior film di Fellini. 3 Non si
sono accorti che ero stanchissimo/a. 4 Qual è il più grande

teatro del mondo? 5 Non mi piace la musica tanto quanto [come] a te. 6 Gli alberghi sono più cari in agosto che in giugno. 7 Ci troviamo tra tre ore? 8 Mi dispiace molto di essere in ritardo. 9 Si è divertita/o con i suoi amici ieri? 10 È riuscito/a a trovare i biglietti?

Week 9

Exercise 83: 1 Gestisce un bar. 2 È quella che parla con Tina e Mario. 3 Marco è un esperto di elettronica. 4 Lavora per una compagnia che fabbrica computer. 5 No, è María che fa l'avvocato.

Exercise 84: 1 che 2 cui 3 cui 4 quello che 5 Quelli che 6 che 7 quello che 8 la quale 9 cui 10 Chi

Exercise 85: 1 Dà del tu ai giovani della sua età e ai parenti. 2 Perchè la conosce da quand'era bambina. 3 Alla cameriera della mensa. 4 Alle persone decisamente più vecchie di lui. 5 No, gli dà del tu.

Exercise 86: 1 Dammi quell'indirizzo! 2 Falle vedere l'ufficio! 3 Dicci la verità! 4 Valla a trovare domani! 5 Dammi del tu! 6 Stacci un po' di più. 7 Falle il biglietto! 8 Dimmi chi è! 9 Fagli una fotografia! 10 Dammi la mano!

Exercise 87: 1 No, sta salendo. 2 No, è di sinistra. 3 Perchè prendono uno stipendio basso [di 700 euro al mese]. 4 Sì, sta salendo. 5 Stanno parlando de altualità.

Exercise 88: 1 guardando 2 Studiando 3 Leggendo 4 mettendo 5 venendo 6 vendendo 7 arrivando 8 discutendo 9 Facendo 10 dicendo

Exercise 89: 1 stanno per 2 sta per 3 stanno per 4 sta per 5 stanno per 6 sta per 7 stanno per 8 stanno per 9 sta per 10 stanno per

Exercise 90:
Italy has been a republic since 1946, when there was a referendum to decide whether to keep the monarchy. The monarchy lost and the Royal Family, the House of Savoy, went into exile.

The constitution, approved in 1948, decrees that the President is Head of State but not Head of the Government: he is elected by Parliament, not by the people.

The Head of Government is the President of the Council of Ministers, with whom he/she, forms the Government. This government must have the approval of both Houses.

Parliament consists of the Chamber of Deputies with 630 members and the Senate with 315. The Chamber of Deputies and the Senate are elected for five years, the President of the Republic for seven years.

Italians have the vote at the age of 18 for the parliamentary elections, but for the Senate the minimum voting age is 25.

Exercise 91: 1 No, è una repubblica dal 1946. 2 No, è Capo dello Stato. 3 Ci sono 630 deputati. 4 Votano a diciotto anni per la Camera e a venticinque per il Senato. 5 Ci sono 315 senatori.

Exercise 92: 1 Dammi le valigie, il treno sta per arrivare. 2 Non sapendo niente, non ho parlato. 3 Non avendo un passaporto, non posso partire. 4 Non può venire adesso perchè sta mangiando. 5 Dimmi chi è! 6 Vacci subito! 7 Non scelgo mai il posto vicino al finestrino. 8 Fa così caldo oggi, sto per svenire. 9 Non posso invitarli, stanno per uscire. 10 Non conoscevo la gente con cui stava.

Week 10

Exercise 93: 1 Vanno in gita in montagna. 2 Sì, dovranno camminare per circa due ore. 3 Arriveranno verso le undici. 4 Fa l'infermiera. 5 Silvana lavora a Milano e Jeff e Tony lavorano a Londra.

Exercise 94: 1 Primo o poi verrò. 2 Prima o poi pagherò. 3 Prima o poi ballerò. 4 Prima o poi andrò. 5 Prima o poi giocherò. 6 Prima o poi sceglierò. 7 Prima o poi finirò. 8 Prima o poi ordinerò. 9 Prima o poi ritonerò. 10 Prima o poi studierò.

Exercise 95: 1 Magari verranno a piedi. 2 Magari dormiremo in tenda. 3 Magari porterete voi qualcosa da mangiare. 4 Magari usciremo più tardi. 5 Magari farà più bella figura. 6 Magari non gli daranno la mancia. 7 Magari ci aspetteranno all'altra fermata. 8 Magari canterò un'altra aria. 9 Magari pagherai tutto insieme. 10 Magari gestirà lui il ristorante.

Exercise 96: 1 Tony lavora in ospedale da tre anni, ma Jeff da due. 2 Fa quattro o cinque turni alla settimana. 3 Perchè non hanno sempre gli stessi turni. 4 Sì, le piace. 5 Gli piace far collezione di francobolli.

Exercise 97: 1 di 2 da 3 di 4 da 5 di 6 alla 7 al 8 alle 9 da 10 a, dalla

Exercise 98: 1 Li ha presi in prestito da Gianni. 2 Li danno a nolo in un negozio di fianco alla Posta. 3 Piove. 4 Si fermeranno al ristorante sopra alla funivia. 5 Si trovano di fronte a casa di Luisa.

Exercise 99: 1 Scriverai davvero a lui? 2 Guardo lui non lei. 3 Parla a noi, ma non a nessun altro. 4 Siete sicuri che scriverà a voi? 5 C'è molta gente prima di lui. 6 Manderai solo un regalo a lei? 7 Parlano spesso di loro. 8 Fa tutto da sè. 9 Andiamo a cavallo con loro. 10 Invitano proprio me?

Exercise 100: 1 Vi scriveremo presto. 2 Ci conosciamo da tre anni. 3 Hanno comprato una cravatta di seta per il loro padre. 4 Faccio l'infermiere/a a Firenze. 5 Hai molto da fare? 6 Voglio vedere te, non la tua ragazza! 7 Comincerò a studiare la settimana prossima. 8 Sono andati a cena da María. 9 Beata/o Lei! 10 L'ospedale è di fronte alla banca.

Mini-dictionary

a to, at, in
abbastanza quite, enough
abitare to live
accessori, (m. pl.) accessories
accettare to accept
accomodarsi make oneself comfortable
accordo (m.) agreement
accórgersene to notice
accórgersi to realize
acqua (f.) water
addormentarsi to fall asleep
adesso now
aéreo (m.) aeroplane
aeroporto (m.) airport
affari (m. pl.) business
affettuoso affectionate, loving
affittare to let, to rent
affitto (m.) rent
affollato crowded
aglio (m.) garlic
agnello (m.) lamb
agosto (m.) August
aiutare to help
aiuto (m.) help
albergo (m.) hotel
alcuni/e (pl.) some, any
al di sotto below
allegro cheerful
allora then
almeno at least
alto high, tall
altrimenti otherwise
alzarsi to get up
ambulanza (f.) ambulance
ambulatorio (m.) surgery
ammalarsi to fall ill
ammalato ill, sick
ammobiliato furnished
analcólico non-alcoholic
anche also, too, as well
ancora still, again, yet
andare to go
andare a trovare to pay a visit

animale (m.) animal
anno (m.) year
annoiarsi to get bored
antipasto (m.) hors d'oeuvre
antipasto misto (m.) hors d'oeuvre of cold meats
anziano old
aperitivo (m.) aperitif
aperto open
appartamento (m.) flat
appassionato fond
approvare to approve
appuntamento (m.) appointment
appunto precisely
aprile (m.) April
aprire to open
arancia (f.) orange
arrabbiarsi to get angry
arrabbiato angry
arrivare to arrive
arrivederci bye-bye
arrivederLa goodbye
arrossamento (m.) reddening
arrosto (m.) roast
artícolo (m.) article
artista (m. & f.) artist
artístico artistic
asciugarsi to get dry
ascoltare to listen
aspettare to wait for
aspirapólvere (m.) vacuum cleaner
assaggiare to taste
assegno (m.) cheque
assenza (f.) absence
atténdere to wait
attento careful
áttimo (m.) minute, moment
attore (m.) actor
attraversare to cross
attrice (f.) actress
attualità (f.) current affairs
aumento (m.) increase
áutobus (m.) bus

automóbile (f.) car
autostrada (f.) motorway
avér caldo to be hot
avere to have
avér fame to be hungry
avér freddo to be cold
avér fretta to be in a hurry
avér male di ... to have a
  pain in ...
avér paura to be afraid
avér ragione to be right
avér sete to be thirsty
avér torto to be wrong
avér voglia to feel like, to want
avvisare to warn
avvocato (m.) lawyer

bagno (m.) bathroom
balcone (m.) balcony
bambino (m.) child
barba (f.) beard
basso low
basta it is enough
beato! lucky! [blessed]
bello beautiful
bene well
benvenuto welcome
benzina (f.) petrol
bere to drink
bianchería (f.) linen
bianco white
bíbita (f.) [soft] drink
biblioteca (f.) library
bicchiere (m.) glass
bicicletta (f.) bicycle
biglietto (m.) ticket
bistecca (f.) steak
blù blue
blusa (f.) blouse
borsa (f.) bag
Borsa (f.) Stock Exchange
borsetta (f.) handbag
braccio (m.) arm
braciola (f.) chop
bravo good, clever
brutto ugly, bad

bufala/o buffalo
buonanotte good night
buonasera good evening
buongiorno good morning
buono (m.) voucher
buono good

cadere to fall
caffè (m.) coffee
caffè corretto (m.) coffee with a
  dash of spirit
calcio (m.) football
caldo hot, warm
calzature (f. pl.) footwear
cambiare to change
cámera (f.) bedroom, room
Cámera (f.) Chamber
cámera da letto (m.) bedroom
cameriere/a waiter/waitress
camicia (f.) shirt
camminare to walk
camminata (f.) walk
campagna (f.) country
campeggio (m.) campsite
cantante (m. & f.) singer
cantare to sing
canzone (f.) song
capire to understand
capítolo (m.) chapter
capo (m.) head, boss
Capo dello Stato (m.) Head of
  State
caraffa (f.) caraffe
carne (f.) meat
caro dear, expensive
carta (f.) map, paper
carta di crédito (f.) credit card
cartina (f.) map
cartolina (f.) postcard
casa (f.) home, house
casetta (f.) small house, cottage
cassetta delle léttere (f.) letter
  box
cassiere/a cashier
catálogo (m.) catalogue
cattivo bad

cavallo (m.) horse
cena (f.) dinner, supper
cenare to dine
cento hundred
centro (m.) centre
cercare to look for
cerniera (f.) zip
centesimo (m.) cent
certo sure, certainly
che that, what, who, whom
che cosa what
chi who?, the one/ones who
chiamare to call
chiamarsi to call oneself, to
   be called
chiave (f.) key
chiédere to ask
chiesa (f.) church
chilo (m.) kilo
chilómetro (m.) kilometre
chiúdere to close
chiuso closed
ciao hello, goodbye
cínema (m.) cinema
cinquanta fifty
cinque five
cioccolatini (m. pl.) chocolates
cioccolato (m.) chocolate
ciò che what, that which
cioè that is (i.e.)
circa about, approximately
città (f.) city, town
ci vuole it takes
coalizione (f.) coalition
coda (f.) queue
códice segreto (m.) PIN number
cógliere to pick
cognome (m.) surname
coincidenza (f.) coincidence
colazione (f.) breakfast
collezione (f.) collection
colore (m.) colour
colpa (f.) fault
come how, like
come mai? how come?, why?
come no yes, certainly (and how)

commesso/a shop assistant
cómodo comfortable
compagnia (f.) company
compagno/a companion, mate,
   partner
cómpere (f. pl.) shopping,
   purchase
cómpito (m.) homework
comprare to buy
comune common
comunista communist
con with
conóscere to know
consigliare to advise
consistere to consist
contento happy
conto (m.) bill
contorno (m.) side dish
contratto (m.) contract
coricarsi to lie down
córrere to run
corridoio (m.) corridor
corso (m.) road, high street
cosa what?, thing
così so
costare to cost
costo (m.) cost
costruire to build
cotoletta (f.) veal cutlet
cotoletta alla milanese (f.) veal
   cutlet coated in breadcrumbs
cotone (m.) cotton
cotto cooked
cravatta (f.) tie
crédere to think
crema (f.) cream
criticare to criticize
cucina (f.) kitchen
cucinare to cook
cui whom, which
cuócere to cook
cúpola (f.) dome
curare to cure
da from, by
dappertutto everywhere
dare to give

dare del tu/del Lei to use **tu/Lei**
dare la mano to shake hands
da solo alone
data (f.) date
davanti a in front of
davvero really
decídere to decide
decisamente definitely
dedicarsi to devote oneself
delicato delicate
democrático democratic
dentista (f. & m.) dentist
dentro inside
deputato (m.) Member of
  Parliament
destra right
desiderare to wish
di of
dicembre (m.) December
diciannove nineteen
di dove? where from?
dieci ten
dieta (f.) diet
dietro a behind
differenza (f.) difference
difficile difficult
difficoltà (f.) difficulty
di fronte a opposite
digitare to punch
dimenticarsi to forget
dipéndere to depend
di più more
di preciso exactly
dire to say
direttore (m.) director, manager
direttrice (f.) director, manager
diritto straight
disastro (m.) disaster
discútere to discuss
di sólito usually
dispiacere to be sorry
distanza (f.) distance
distinto distinguished
distratto absent-minded, distracted
disturbare to bother
disturbo (m.) bother

dito (m.) finger, toe
ditta (f.) firm
di turno on duty
diventare to become
diversi (pl.) several
diverso different
divertirsi to enjoy oneself
divisa (f.) uniform
doccia (f.) shower
documento (m.) document
dódici twelve
domandare to ask
domani tomorrow
doménica (f.) Sunday
dopo after, later, then
doppio double
dormire to sleep
dottore (m.) doctor
dottoressa (f.) doctor
dove where
dovere to have to, must
droghiere/a grocer
due two
dunque so, then
duomo (m.) cathedral
durare to last
durata (f.) duration
duro hard

e and
eccetto except
ecco here is, here it is
eléggere to elect
elettrónica (f.) electronics
elezioni (f. pl.) elections
ente (m.) body, organization, board
entrare in vigore to become law
esaminare to examine
esilio (m.) exile
esperto/a expert
esporsi al sole to sunbathe
espressivo intense, with feeling
éssere to be
éssere abituato a to be used to
éssere nato to be born
est (m.) east

estate (f.) summer
età (f.) age
etto (m.) 100 grammes
euro (m. sing.) euro
evitare to avoid
extra extra

fabbricare to manufacture
facchino (m.) porter
fácile easy
facilmente easily
fame (f.) hunger
famiglia (f.) family
famoso famous
fantástico great
far bella figura to look good, to
  impress
fárcela to manage, to cope
far conoscenza to get acquainted
fare to do, to make
farmacía (f.) pharmacy, chemist's
farmacista (m. & f.) chemist
far male to hurt
far vedere to show
fatica (f.) effort
febbraio (m.) February
febbre (f.) temperature, fever
fermarsi to stop, to stay
fermata (f.) stop
ferroviere (m.) railman
festa (f.) feast (day), party
figlia (f.) daughter
figlio (m.) son, child
figura (f.) figure
figúrati you are welcome (fam.)
finalmente at last
finchè ... non until
finestra (f.) window
finire to finish
fino a as far as
finocchio (m.) fennel
Firenze (f.) Florence
fissare to arrange
foglio (m.) sheet of paper
forma (f.) form, shape
formare to form

forno (m.) oven
forse perhaps
fortunato lucky
francobollo (m.) stamp
fratello (m.) brother
freddo (m.) cold
fresco fresh
fretta (f.) hurry
frizzante fizzy
frutta (f.) fruit
fruttivéndolo/a greengrocer
fumare to smoke
funivía (f.) cable car
funzionare to work, function
fuori outside

gabinetto (m.) lavatory, toilet
gallería (f.) gallery
gamba (f.) leg
garage (m.) garage
gastroenterite (f.) gastroenteritis
gelato (m.) ice cream
gelato frozen
generale general
genio (m.) genius
genitori (m. pl.) parents
gennaio (m.) January
Génova (f.) Genoa
gente (f. sing.) people
gentile kind
gestire to run (a business)
già already
giardino (m.) garden
ginocchio (m.) knee
giocare to play (a game)
giornalaio/a newsagent
giornale (m.) newspaper
giorno (m.) day
gióvane young
giovedì (m.) Thursday
gita (f.) trip
giugno (m.) June
giusto correct
gnocchi (m. pl.) potato dumplings
gnocchi alla romana (m. pl.)
  semolina dumplings

governo (m.) government
grado (m.) degree
grande big
grata (f.) shutter
gratis free
grazie thank you
griglia (f.) grill
grissino (m.) breadstick
guardare to see
guida (f.) guide, guide book
guidare to drive

hobby (m.) hobby

idea (f.) idea
ieri yesterday
ignorare to ignore
il (m.) the
il quale who, whom,
   which, that
imbucare to post
imparare to learn
impegnato busy, engaged
impiegato/a clerk
importante important
impostare to post in in
incidente (m.) accident
in cima a on top of
incontrarsi to meet
indietro back
indirizzo (m.) address
indisposto indisposed, unwell
infermiere/a nurse
inflazione (f.) inflation
in fondo a at the end of
informazione (f.) information
Inghilterra (f.) England
inglese (m. & f.) English
in orario on time
in pensione retired
inquilino/a tenant
in ritardo late, delayed
insalata (f.) salad
insegnante (m. & f.) teacher
insieme a together with
insistere to insist

insuperábile unmatched,
   outstanding
intelligente intelligent, clever
inténdere to understand
interessarsi to be interested
interno (m.) interior
interrómpere to interrupt
in tutto altogether
invece instead
inverno (m.) winter
investire to run over
invitare to invite
invito (m.) invitation
istituto (m.) institute, faculty
Italia (f.) Italy
italiano/a Italian

la (f.) the
labbro (m.) lip
laburista labour
lana (f.) wool
lasagne (f. pl.) lasagne
lasciare to leave
laterale on the side
lavandería (f.) wash house,
   launderette
lavapiatti (f.) dishwasher
lavarsi to wash oneself
lavatrice (f.) washing machine
lavorare to work
lavoro (m.) work
leggero light, mild
legno (m.) wood
lei she
Lei you (formal)
léttera (f.) letter
lettino (m.) couch
letto (m.) bed
lezione (f.) lesson
li there
liberale liberal
líbero free
lingua (f.) language
lírica (f.) operatic music
lista (f.) list
Londra (f.) London

lontano da far from
luce light
luglio (m.) July
lunedì (m.) Monday

ma but
madre (f.) mother
magari perhaps
maglione (m.) sweater
maiale (m.) pig, pork
mácchina (f.) car, machine
maggio (m.) May
maggiore greater, greatest,
    older, oldest
magnífico magnificent
malattía (f.) illness, disease
male badly
mamma (f.) mum, mummy
mancia (f.) tip
mandare to send
mangiare to eat
mano (f.) hand
mantenere to keep
manzo (m.) beef
mare (m.) sea
marito (m.) husband
martedì (m.) Tuesday
marzo (m.) March
matita (f.) pencil
mattino (m.) morning
media (f.) average
medicina (f.) medicine
médico (m.) (medical) doctor
meglio better (adv.)
membro (m.) member
meno less, least
meno male thank goodness
mensa (f.) refectory, canteen
mercato (m.) market
mercoledì (m.) Wednesday
mese (m.) month
metropolitana (f.) underground
méttere to put
mezzanotte (f.) midnight
mezzo half, means
mezzogiorno (m.) midday

mi dispiace I am sorry
migliore better, best
Milano (f.) Milan
milione (m.) million
mille thousand
mille grazie many thanks
minerale mineral
minestra (f.) soup
mínimo minimum
minore smaller/-est, younger/-est
minuto (m.) minute
mio my, mine
mi pare I think
mi piace I like
mi raccomando! mind!
misura (f.) size
móbili (m. pl.) furniture
moderno modern
moglie (f.) wife
molto very, much
molto lieto pleased (to meet you)
momento (m.) moment
monarchía (f.) monarchy
mondo (m.) world
montagna (f.) mountain
monte (m.) mount, mountain
morire to die
morto dead
mosso rough (sea)
mostra (f.) exhibition
motocicletta (f.) motorbike
motorino (m.) scooter
mucca (f.) cow
muscolare muscular
música (f.) music

Nápoli (f.) Naples
nato born
nazionale national
neanche neither, not even
necessario necessary
negozio (m.) shop
nel frattempo in the meantime
nessuno/a nobody
niente nothing
no no

noioso boring
noleggiare to hire
noleggio, nolo (m.) hire
non not
non vedér l'ora di to look
    forward to
nome (m.) name
nord (m.) north
notizie (f. pl.) news
notte (f.) night
novanta ninety
nove nine
novembre (m.) November
número (m.) number
nuotare to swim
nuovo new
obbligatorio compulsory
occasione (f.) opportunity
occhiali (m. pl.) spectacles
occhiata (f.) look
occupato busy
occupazione (f.) occupation
offrire to offer
oggi today
ogni every
olio (m.) oil
oliva (f.) olive
ópera (f.) opera
ora (f.) hour
orario (m.) timetable
ordinare to order
orecchio (m.) ear
orologiaio/a watchmaker
ospedale (m.) hospital
óspite (m. & f.) guest
ostería (f.) bar
ottanta eighty
otto eight
ottobre (m.) October
ovest (m.) west

padre (m.) father
padrona [di casa] (f.) landlady
padrone [di casa] (m.) landlord
pane (m.) bread
panino (m.) bread roll, sandwich

pantófole (f. pl.) slippers
Papa (m.) Pope
papà (m.) dad
parente (m. & f.) relative
parlamentare parliamentary
Parlamento (m.) Parliament
parlare to speak
parmigiano (m.) parmesan
partire to leave
partita (f.) match
partito (m.) (political) party
passaporto (m.) passport
passare to pass
passatempo (m.) pastime
passeggero (m.) passenger
passeggiata (f.) walk
passione (f.) passion, interest
pastina (f.) little cake
pasto (m.) meal
patata (f.) potato
patate fritte (f. pl.) chips
paura (f.) fear
Pavía (f.) Pavia
paziente patient
pazzo mad
peggio worse (adv.)
peggiore worse/worst
pelle (f.) leather
pensare to think
pensionante (m. & f.) paying
    guest
pensionato/a retired
pensione completa (f.) full board
per for
per cento per cent
perchè why, because
pérdere to lose
pérdersi to get lost
per esempio for example
per favore/per piacere please
perifería (f.) suburbs
perméttere to allow
personale personal
per terra on the floor/ground
pesce (m.) fish
péssimo very bad

pezzo (m.) piece
piacere how do you do, pleasure
piacévole pleasant
piángere to weep, to cry
pianista (m & f.) pianist
piano (m.) floor
piano slowly
piano, pianoforte (m.) piano
pianterreno (m.) ground floor
piantina (f.) map
piatto (m.) dish
piazza (f.) square
píccolo small
piedi (m. pl.) feet
pieno full
piscina (f.) swimming pool
poco little
poi then
Policlínico (m.) General Hospital
Politécnico (m.) polytechnic
política (f.) politics
pomata (f.) ointment
pomeriggio (m.) afternoon
pomodoro (m.) tomato
pópolo (m.) people
porta (f.) door
portare to carry, to wear
portare di ritorno/indietro
  to take back
portavoce (m. & f.) spokesperson
portinaio/a doorkeeper
possíbile possible
posta (f.) mail/post office
posto (m.) seat, place
potere to be able
póvero poor
pranzo (m.) lunch
preciso precise
preferire to prefer
preferito favourite
pregare to pray, to beg
prego you are welcome, please
prémere to press
préndere to take
préndere in préstito to borrow
prenotare to book

preoccuparsi to worry
preparare to prepare
prescrívere to prescribe
presentare to introduce
presidente (m.) president,
  chairperson
Presidente del Consiglio
  Prime Minister
prestare to lend
préstito (m.) loan
presto early
presuntuoso conceited
Pretura (f.) Police Headquarters
prezzo (m.) price
prima colazione (f.) breakfast
prima di before
primo first
primo piatto (m.) first course
probabilmente probably
programma (m.) programme
pronto soccorso (m.) A & E
proprietario/a owner
proprio really, quite
prosciutto (m.) ham
próssimo next
protettivo protective
pulire to clean
purtroppo unfortunately

quanto how, how much
qualche some
qualcosa something
qual(e) what, which
qualsíasi whatever, any
qualunque whatever, any
quando when
quaranta forty
quarto fourth
quattórdici fourteen
quattro four
questione (f.) matter,
  question
questo this
qui here
quíndici fifteen
quotidiano daily

rádersi to shave
radio (f.) radio
ragazza (f.) girl, girlfriend
ragazzo (m.) boy, boyfriend
ragione (f.) right, reason
recitare to act
reclami (m. pl.) complaints
referendum (m.) referendum
regalare to give (as a present)
regalo (m.) present
regata (f.) regatta
regionale regional
regione (f.) region
regnante ruling
reparto (m.) department
repúbblica (f.) republic
repubblicano republican
restare to stay, to remain
restaurare to restore
ricetta (f.) prescription
ricévere to receive
ricevuta (f.) receipt
riconóscere to recognize
ricordarsi to remember
ricotta (f.) cream cheese
rifiutare to refuse
riga (f.) stripe, line
rilassarsi to relax
rimanere to stay
rimborso (m.) refund
rimodernare to modernize
riparare to mend
riposarsi to rest
riservare to book
risparmiare to save
rispóndere to reply
ristorante (m.) restaurant
ritardo (m.) delay
riuscire to succeed
rivedere to see again
rivista (f.) magazine
roba (f.) belongings, things
rómpere to break
rosso red
roulotte (f.) caravan
rumore (m.) noise

russo Russian
rústico (m.) farmhouse
sábato (m.) Saturday
salotto (m.) lounge, drawing room
sala da pranzo (m.) dining room
salame (m.) salami
salire to climb, to go up
salutare to greet
salute (f.) health, cheers!
sapere to know how
sbagliato wrong
scarpe (f. pl.) shoes
scarponi (m. pl.) boots
scátola (f.) box
scégliere to choose
scéndere to go down, to descend
scelta (f.) choice
schermo (m.) screen
schiena (f.) back
sci (m. pl.) skis
sciare to ski
sciógliere to dissolve
sciópero (m.) strike
scompartimento (m.)
  compartment
scottatura (f.) burn
scrivanía (f.) desk
scrívere to write
scuola (f.) school
scuola elementare (f.)
  elementary school
scuola media (f.) middle school
scusa (f.) excuse
scusare to excuse, to forgive
se if, whether
secco dry
sécolo (m.) century
secondo according to, in the
  opinion of
secondo second
sedersi to sit down
sédici sixteen
segretario/a secretary
segreto secret
seguire to follow
sei six

semáforo (m.) traffic lights
sempre always
Senato (m.) Senate
senatore (m.) senator
senso (m.) way, sense
sentire to hear
sentirsi to feel
serio serious
servire to serve
servizi (m. pl.) facilities
servizio (m.) set
sessanta sixty
sesto sixth
seta (f.) silk
sete (f.) thirst
settanta seventy
sette seven
settembre (m.) September
settimana (f.) week
sgabuzzino (m.) closet
sgonfio flat (tyre)
si one, oneself, him/herself,
  themselves
sì yes
sicuro sure
sì e no hardly
signora (f.) Mrs, madam, Ms
signore (m.) Mr, sir
signorina (f.) Miss, young lady
simpático likeable
sincero sincere
sindacato (m.) trade union
síngolo single
sinistra left
sistema (m.) system
socialista socialist
soggiorno (m.) stay, living room
soldi (m.) (pl.) money
sole (m.) sun
solo only
soprattutto mainly
sorella (f.) sister
sotto below, under
spaghetti (m. pl.) spaghetti
Spagna (f.) Spain
spazioso roomy

specialità (f.) speciality
specialmente specially
spellarsi to peel
spéndere to spend
spesa (f.) shopping
spesso often
spettácolo (m.) show, spectacle
spettatore (m.) spectator
spiegare to explain
sporcarsi to get dirty
sporco dirty
sportello (m.) (train) door
sposarsi to get married
stabilire to establish, to dictate
stadio (m.) stadium
stamattina this morning
stancarsi to get tired
stanco tired
stanza (f.) room
stazione (f.) station
stesso the same
stómaco (m.) stomach
storia (f.) story, history
stórico historical
strada (f.) road
straniero/a foreign, foreigner
strappo (m.) sprain
studente (m.) student
studiare to study
studioso studious
stúpido stupid
su on
súbito immediately
succédere to happen
sud (m.) south
suo his/hers, yours (form.)
suócera (f.) mother-in-law
suonare to play (an instrument),
  to ring
supermercato (m.) supermarket
svago (m.) pastime
svegliarsi to wake up
svéndita (f.) sale
svestirsi to undress

tabaccaio/a (m.) tobacconist

tanto ... quanto as ... as
tardi late
tartina (f.) canapé
tassa di soggiorno (f.) tourist tax
taxi (m.) taxi
teatro (m.) theatre
telefonare to phone
teléfono (m.) telephone
telegramma (m.) telegramme
televisione (f.) television
tenda (f.) tent
tenere to keep, to hold
tenore (m.) tenor
terrazzo (m.) terrace
tesi (f.) thesis
testa (f.) head
tifo (m.) (fare il tifo per)
   to support
tifoso (m.) fan, supporter
tinello (m.) breakfast room
tocca a me it is my turn
tornare to go/come back, to return
torto (m.) wrong
tra among, between
trágico tragic
trasporto (m.) transport
tre three
trédici thirteen
treno (m.) train
trenta thirty
troppo too, too much
trota (f.) trout
trovare to find
trovarsi to meet
turno (m.) duty

un, una a, an
úndici eleven
ufficio (m.) office
ufficio postale (m.) post office
uguale same, equal
único unique
università (f.) university
uno one
un po' a little
usare to use

uscire to go out
vacanza (f.) holiday
vagone (m.) carriage
valigia (f.) suitcase
vecchio old
vedere to see
vegetariano vegetarian
véndita (f.) sale
venerdì (m.) Friday
Venezia (f.) Venice
venire to come
vend twenty
veramente really
verde green
verdura (f.) vegetable
verità (f.) truth
vero true
vestirsi to get dressed
vestito (m.) dress, suit
vettura (f.) carriage
viaggiare to travel
vicino near
violinista (m. & f.) violinist
vísita (f.) visit
visitare to visit, to examine
viso (m.) face
vita (f.) life
vitello (m.) veal
voce (f.) voice
voglia (f.) wish
volentieri willingly
volere to want, to wish
volo (m.) flight
volta (f.) time
votare to vote
voto (m.) vote
vuoto empty

weekend (m.) weekend

zanzara (f.) mosquito
zero (m.) zero, nought
zia (f.) aunt
zio (m.) uncle
zoo (m.) zoo
zúcchero (m.) sugar

a, an un, una, uno
a little un po'
absence assenza (f.)
to accept accettare
accessories accessori (m. pl.)
accident incidente (m.)
according to secondo
to act recitare
actor attore (m.)
actress attrice (f.)
address indirizzo (m.)
advice consiglio (m.)
to advise consigliare
aeroplane aeroplano, aéreo (m.)
affectionate affettuoso
after dopo, poi
afternoon pomeriggio (m.)
again ancora
age età (f.)
agreement accordo (m.)
airport aeroporto (m.)
to allow perméttere
alone da solo
already già
also anche
altogether in tutto
always sempre
ambulance ambulanza (f.)
among fra, tra
and e
angry arrabbiato
animal animale (m.)
any alcuni, qualsíasi, qualunque
aperitif aperitivo (m.)
appointment appuntamento (m.)
to approve approvare
approximately circa
April aprile (m.)
arm braccio (m.)
to arrange fissare
to arrive arrivare
article artíicolo (m.)
artist artista (m. & f.)
artistic artístico
as ... as tanto ... quanto

as far as fino a
to ask chiédere, domandare
as well anche
at a, in
at last finalmente
at least almeno
at the end of in fondo a
aunt zia (f.)
August agosto (m.)
average media (f.)
to avoid evitare

back schiena (f.)
bad cattivo, brutto
badly male
bag borsa (f.)
balcony balcone (m.)
bank banca (f.)
bar ostería (f.)
bathroom bagno (m.)
to be éssere
to be afraid avere paura
to be born éssere nato
to be called chiamarsi
to be cold avere freddo
to be hot avere caldo
to be hungry avere fame
to be in a hurry avere fretta
to be right avere ragione
to be thirsty avere sete
to be used to éssere abituato a
to be wrong avere torto
beard barba (f.)
beautiful bello
because perchè
because of a causa di
to become diventare
to become law entrare in vigore
bed letto (m.)
bedroom cámera da letto (m.)
beef manzo (m.)
before prima di
to beg pregare
to begin cominciare
behind dietro a

to believe crédere
belongings roba (f.)
below sotto
beside a fianco di
better (adv) meglio
better, best migliore
between fra, tra
bicycle bicicletta (f.)
big grande
bill conto (m.)
blouse blusa (f.)
blue blù
board ente (m.)
boarding house pensione (f.)
to book prenotare, riservare
boots scarponi (m. pl.)
boring noioso
born nato
to borrow préndere in préstito
boss capo (m.)
to bother disturbare
box scátola (f.)
boy ragazzo (m.)
boyfriend ragazzo (m.)
bread pane (m.)
bread roll panino (m.)
to break rómpere
breakfast colazione (f.)
breakfast room tinello (m.)
brother fratello (m.)
buffalo búfalo/a
to build costruire
burn scottatura (f.)
bus áutobus (m.)
business affari (m.) (pl.)
busy occupato, impegnato
but ma
to buy comprare
by da
bye-bye arrivederci

cable car funivía, funicolare (f.)
cake [little] pastina (f.)
to call chiamare
to call oneself chiamarsi
campsite campeggio (m.)

can potere
canapé tartina (f.)
canteen mensa (f.)
car automóbile, mácchina (f.)
carafe caraffa (f.)
caravan roulotte (f.)
careful attento
to be careful stare attento
carriage vagone (m.), vettura (f.)
carry portare
cashier cassiere/a
casualty pronto soccorso (m.)
catalogue catálogo (m.)
cathedral duomo (m.)
cent centesimo (m.)
centre centro (m.)
century sécolo (m.)
certainly certo
Chamber Cámera (f.)
to change cambiare
chapter capítolo (m.)
cheerful allegro
cheers! salute!
chemist farmacista (m. & f.)
chemist's farmacía (f.)
cheque assegno (m.)
child bambino/a
chocolate cioccolato (m.)
chocolates cioccolatini (m. pl.)
choice scelta (f.)
to choose scégliere
chop braciola (f.)
church chiesa (f.)
cinema cínema (m.)
city città (f.)
to clean pulire
clever bravo
to climb salire
to close chiúdere
closed chiuso
closet sgabuzzino (m.)
coalition coalizione (f.)
coffee caffè (m.)
coincidence coincidenza (f.)
cold freddo (m.)
collection collezione (f.)

college collegio (m.)
colour colore (m.)
to come venire
comfortable cómodo
companion compagno/a
company compagnia (f.)
compartment scompartimento (m.)
complaint reclamo (m.)
compulsory obbligatorio
conceited presuntuoso
to consist consístere
contract contratto (m.)
to cook cucinare, cuócere
cooked cotto
to cope fárcela
correct giusto
corridor corridoio (m.)
cost costo (m.)
to cost costare
cottage casetta (f.)
cotton cotone (m.)
couch lettino (m.)
countryside campagna (f.)
course (dish) piatto (m.)
cow mucca (f.)
cream crema (f.)
credit card carta di crédito (f.)
to criticize criticare
to cross attraversare
crowded affollato
to cure curare
current affairs attualità (f.)

dad, daddy papà, babbo (m.)
daily quotidiano
date data (f.)
daughter figlia (f.)
day giorno (m.)
dead morto
December dicembre (m.)
to decide decídere
definitely decisamente
degree grado (m.)
delicate delicato
democratic democrático
dentist dentista (m. & f.)

department reparto (m.)
to depend dipéndere
desk scrivanía (f.)
to devote oneself dedicarsi
to dictate stabilire
to die morire
diet dieta (f.)
difference differenza (f.)
different diverso
difficult difficile
difficulty difficoltà (f.)
to dine cenare
dining room sala da pranzo (f.)
dinner cena (f.)
director direttore m, direttrice (f.)
dirty sporco
to get dirty sporcarsi
to discuss discútere
dish piatto (m.)
dishwasher lavapiatti (f.)
to dissolve sciógliere
distance distanza (f.)
distracted distratto
to do fare
doctor médico (m.), dottore/-ssa
document documento (m.)
dome cúpola (f.)
door porta (f.)
door bell campanello (m.)
doorkeeper portinaio/a
double doppio
dress vestito (m.)
to get dressed vestirsi
drink (soft) bíbita (f.)
to drink bere
dry secco
to dry oneself asciugarsi
dumplings gnocchi (m. pl.)
duration durata
duty turno (m.)
on duty di turno

ear orecchio (m.)
early presto
easily facilmente
east est (m.)

easy fácile
to eat mangiare
effort fática
eight otto
eighteen diciotto
eighty ottanta
to elect eléggere
elections elezioni (f. pl.)
electronics elettrónica (f.)
elementary school scuola elementare (f.)
eleven úndici
empty vuoto
England Inghilterra (f.)
English inglese (m. & f.)
to enjoy oneself divertirsi
enough abbastanza
equal uguale
to establish stabilire
euro euro (m.)
eventually alla fine
every ogni
everywhere dappertutto
exactly di preciso
examination esame (m.)
to examine esaminare
except eccetto
excuse scusa (f.)
to excuse, to forgive scusare
exhibition mostra (f.)
exile esilio (m.)
expensive caro
expert esperto/a
to explain spiegare

face viso (m.), faccia (f.)
facilities servizi (m. pl.)
to fall cadere
to fall ill ammalarsi
family famiglia (f.)
famous famoso
fantastic fantástico
far from lontano da
farmhouse fattoría (f.), rústico (m.)
fast veloce

father padre (m.)
fault colpa (f.)
favourite preferito
fear paura (f.)
feast festa (f.)
February febbraio (m.)
feel sentirsi
to feel like avér voglia (di)
feet piedi (m. pl.)
fennel finocchio (m.)
fever febbre (f.)
few alcuni, pochi (pl.)
fifteen quíndici
fifty cinquanta
figure figura (f.)
find trovare
finger dito (m.)
to finish finire
firm ditta (f.)
first primo
fish pesce (m.)
five cinque
fizzy frizzante
flat appartamento (m.)
flat (tyre) sgonfio
flight volo (m.)
floor piano (m.)
Florence Firenze (f.)
to follow seguire
fond appassionato
football calcio (m.)
footwear calzature (f. pl.)
for per
foreign, foreigner straniero/a
for example per esempio
to forget dimenticarsi
form forma (f.)
to form formare
forty quaranta
four quattro
fourteen quattórdici
fourth quarto
free líbero
fresh fresco
Friday venerdì (m.)
friend amico (m.) amica (f.)

from da
frozen gelato
fruit frutta (f.)
full pieno
to function funzionare
furnished ammobiliato
furniture móbili (m. pl.)

gallery gallería (f.)
garage garage (m.)
garden giardino (m.)
garlic aglio (m.)
gastroenteritis gastroenterite (f.)
general generale
General Hospital Policlínico (m.)
genius genio (m.)
to get [become] diventare
to get [obtain] ottenere
to get angry arrabbiarsi
to get bored annoiarsi
to get dirty sporcarsi
to get dressed vestirsi
to get dry asciugarsi
to get lost pérdersi
to get married sposarsi
to get tired stancarsi
to get undressed svestirsi
to get up alzarsi
to get worried preoccuparsi
girl ragazza (f.)
girlfriend ragazza (f.)
to give dare
to give (as a present) regalare
glass bicchiere (m.)
to go andare
to go down scéndere
to go out uscire
to go up salire
good buono, bravo
goodbye ciao, arrivederci
good evening buonasera
good morning buongiorno
good night buonanotte
greater, greatest maggiore
green verde
greengrocer fruttivéndolo/a

to greet salutare
grill griglia (f.)
grocer droghiere/a
ground floor pianterreno (m.)
guest óspite (m. & f.)
guide guida (f.)

half mezzo
ham prosciutto (m.)
hand mano (f.)
handbag borsetta (f.)
to happen succédere
happy contento
hard duro
hardly appena, sì e no
to have avere
to have a pain in ... aver male
   di ...
head testa (f.)
Head of State Capo dello Stato
   (m.)
to hear sentire
hello ciao
help aiuto (m.)
to help aiutare
here qui
here it is, here is ecco
high alto
hire noleggio, nolo (m.)
historical stórico
hobby hobby, passatempo (m.)
holiday vacanza (f.)
homework cómpito (m.)
hors d'oeuvre antipasto (m.)
horse cavallo (m.)
hospital ospedale (m.)
hostel ostello (m.)
hot, warm caldo
hotel albergo (m.)
hour ora (f.)
house casa (f.)
how come
how come?, why? come mai?
how do you do piacere
how, how much quanto
hundred cento

hunger fame (m.)
hurry fretta (f.)
to hurry up affrettarsi
to hurt far male
husband marito (m.)

ice cream gelato (m.)
idea idea (f.)
if se
to ignore ignorare
ill ammalato, malato
illness, disease malattía (m.)
immediately súbito
important importante
in in
increase aumento (m.)
inflation inflazione (f.)
information informazione (f.)
in front of davanti a
inside interno (m.), dentro
instead invece
institute istituto (m.)
to introduce presentare
intelligent intelligente
intense, with feeling espressivo
to be interested interessarsi
to interrupt interrómpere
invitation invito (m.)
to invite invitare
Italian italiano
Italy Italia (f.)

January gennaio (m.)
July luglio (m.)
June giugno (m.)

to keep tenere, mantenere
key chiave (f.)
kilo(gramme) chilo (m.)
kilometre chilómetro (m.)
kind gentile
kitchen cucina (f.)
knee ginocchio (m.)
to know conóscere
to know how sapere
labour laburista

lady signora (f.)
lake lago (m.)
lamb agnello (m.)
landlord/landlady padrone/a
language lingua (f.)
lasagne lasagne (f. pl.)
late in ritardo, tardi
launderette lavandería (f.)
lawyer avvocato (m.)
learn imparare
leather pelle (f.)
to leave partire, lasciare
left sinistra
leg gamba (f.)
to lend prestare
less, least meno
lesson lezione (f.)
to let affittare, lasciare
letter léttera (f.)
letter box cassetta delle
  léttere (f.)
liberal liberale
library biblioteca (f.)
to lie down coricarsi
life vita (f.)
light luce (f.)
light leggero
like come
I like mi piace
likeable simpático
line riga (f.)
linen bianchería (f.)
lip labbro (m.)
list lista (f.)
to listen ascoltare
a little un po'
to live abitare
loan préstito (m.)
London Londra (f.)
look occhiata (f.)
to look at guardare
to look for cercare
to look forward to non vedér
  l'ora di
to lose pérdere
lounge salotto (m.)

low basso
lucky fortunato, beato!
lunch pranzo (m.)

mad pazzo
madam signora (f.)
magazine rivista (f.)
magnificent magnífico
mail posta (f.)
mainly soprattutto
to make fare
to manage fárcela
manager direttore/direttrice
to manufacture fabbricare
map cartina, carta, piantina (f.)
March marzo (m.)
market mercato (m.)
marvellous stupendo, meraviglioso
match partita (f.)
matter questione (f.)
May maggio (m.)
maybe forse
meal pasto (m.)
means mezzo (m.)
meanwhile nel frattempo
meat came (f.)
medicine medicina (f.)
to meet incontrarsi, trovarsi
member membro (m.)
Member of Parliament deputato (m.)
to mend riparare
midday mezzogiorno (m.)
middle school scuola media (f.)
midnight mezzanotte (f.)
Milan Milano (f.)
million milione (m.)
mind! mi raccomando!
mine mio
mineral minerale
minimum mínimo
minute minuto (m.)
Miss signorina (f.)
modern moderno
to modernize rimodernare

moment momento (m.), áttimo (m.)
monarchy monarchía (f.)
Monday lunedì (m.)
money soldi (m. pl.)
month mese (m.)
more più, di più
morning mattino (m.)
mosquito zanzara (f.)
mother madre (f.)
mother-in-law suócera (f.)
motorcycle motocicletta (f.)
motorway autostrada (f.)
mount monte (m.)
mountain montagna (f.)
Mr signore (m.)
Mrs signora (f.)
Ms signora (f.)
much molto
mum, mummy mamma (f.)
muscular muscolare
must dovere
my mio

name nome (m.)
national nazionale
near vicino
necessary necessario
new nuovo
news notizie (f. pl.)
newsagent giornalaio/a
newspaper giornale (m.)
next próssimo
next to accanto a, a fianco di
night notte (f.)
nine nove
ninety novanta
no no
nobody nessuno/a
noise rumore (m.)
non-alcoholic analcólico
north nord (m.)
not non
nothing niente, nulla
to notice accórgersene
nought zero (m.)

November novembre
now adesso
number número (m.)
nurse infermiere/a

occupation occupazione (f.)
of di
to offer offrire
office ufficio (m.)
often spesso
oil olio (m.)
ointment pomata (f.)
old vecchio, anziano
olive oliva (f.)
on su
on the side laterale
on top of in cima a
one uno
the one/ones who chi
only solo
open aperto
to open aprire
operatic music lírica (f.)
opportunity occasione (f.)
opposite di fronte a
orange arancia (f.)
to order ordinare
otherwise altrimenti
outside fuori
oven forno (m.)
owner proprietario/a

parents genitori (m. pl.)
Parliament parlamento (m.)
parliamentary parlamentare
parmesan parmigiano (m.)
partner compagno/a
party partito (m.)
to pass passare
passenger passeggero/a
passion passione (f.)
passport passaporto (m.)
pastime svago (m.)
patient paziente
to pay pagare
to pay attention stare attento

paying guest pensionante (m. & f.)
to peel spellarsi
pencil matita (f.)
people pópolo (m.), gente (f.)
per cent per cento
perhaps forse, magari
personal personale
petrol benzina (f.)
pharmacy farmacía (f.)
to phone telefonare
pianist pianista (m. & f.)
piano piano, pianoforte (m.)
to pick cógliere
piece pezzo (m.)
pig maiale (m.)
pin number códice segreto (m.)
place posto (m.)
to play (game) giocare
to play (instrument) suonare
pleasant piacévole, simpático
please per favore, per piacere,
  prego
pleased to meet you molto lieto
politics política (f.)
polytechnic Politécnico (m.)
poor póvero
Pope Papa (m.)
porter facchino (m.)
possible possíbile
to post imbucare, impostare
post office posta (f.), ufficio
  postale (m.)
potato patata (f.)
to pray pregare
precisely appunto
to prefer preferire
to prepare preparare
prescribe prescrívere
prescription ricetta (f.)
present regalo (m.)
president presidente (m.)
to press prémere
price prezzo (m.)
Prime Minister presidente del
  consiglio
probably probabilmente

programme programma (m.)
protective protettivo
to punch in digitare
purchase cómpera (f.)
to put méttere

question questione (f.)
queue coda (f.)
quite abbastanza

radio radio (f.)
railman ferroviere (m.)
to rain pióvere
to realize accórgersi
really proprio, veramente
reason ragione (f.)
receipt ricévuta (f.)
to receive ricévere
to recognize riconóscere
red rosso
reddening arrossamento (m.)
refectory mensa (f.)
referendum referendum (m.)
regatta regata (f.)
region regione (f.)
regional regionale
relative parente (m. & f.)
to remain restare
to remember ricordarsi
rent affitto (m.)
to rent affittare
to reply rispóndere
republic repúbblica (f.)
republican repubblicano
to rest riposarsi
restaurant ristorante (m.)
to restore restaurare
retired in pensione, pensionato/a
right destra
right, reason ragione (f.)
to ring suonare
road strada (f.), via (f.), corso (m.)
roast arrosto (m.)
Rome Roma (f.)
room cámera (f.), stanza (f.)
roomy spazioso

rough (sea) mosso
ruling regnante
to run córrere
to run a business gestire
to run over investire
Russian russo

salad insalata (f.)
salami salame (m.)
sale véndita (f.)
sales svéndita (f.)
same stesso, uguale
Saturday sábato (m.)
to save risparmiare
to say dire
school scuola (f.)
scooter motorino (m.)
screen schermo (m.)
sea mare (m.)
seat posto (m.)
to see vedere
to see again rivedere
second secondo
secret segreto
secretary segretario/a
to sell véndere
Senate Senato (m.)
senator senatore (m.)
to send mandare
sense senso (m.)
September settembre (m.)
serious serio
to serve servire
set servizio (m.)
seven sette
seventeen diciassette
seventy settanta
several diversi (pl.)
to shake hands dare la mano
to shave rádersi
sheet (of paper) foglio (m.)
shirt camicia (f.)
shoes scarpe (f. pl.)
shop negozio (m.)
shop assistant commesso/a
shopping spesa (f.) spese (f. pl.)

to show far vedere
show spettácolo (m.)
shower doccia (f.)
side dish contorno (m.)
silk seta (f.)
sincere sincero
to sing cantare
singer cantante (m. & f.)
single síngolo
sir signore
sister sorella (f.)
to sit down sedersi
six sei
sixteen sédici
sixth sesto
sixty sessanta
size misura (f.)
to ski sciare
skis sci (m. pl.)
to sleep dormire
slippers pantófole (f. pl.)
slowly piano
small piccolo
smaller, smallest minore
to smoke fumare
so così
socialist socialista
soft drink bíbita (f.)
some qualche, alcuni
something qualcosa
son figlio (m.)
sorry scusi, [mi] dispiace
soup minestra (f.)
spaghetti spaghetti (m. pl.)
Spain Spagna (f.)
to speak parlare
speciality specialità
specially specialmente
spectacles occhiali (m. pl.)
spectator spettatore (m.)
to spend spéndere
spokesperson portavoce (m. & f.)
sprain strappo (m.)
square piazza (f.)
stamp francobollo (m.)
station stazione (f.)

to stay rimanere, restare, stare
steak bistecca (f.)
still ancora
Stock Exchange Borsa (f.)
stomach stómaco (m.)
stop fermata (f.)
to stop fermarsi
story storia (f.)
straight diritto
strike sciópero (m.)
stripe riga (f.)
student studente (m.)
studious studioso
to study studiare
stupid stúpido
suburbs perifería (f.)
to succeed riuscire
sugar zúcchero (m.)
suitcase valigia (f.)
summer estate (f.)
sun sole (m.)
to sunbathe esporsi al sole
Sunday doménica (f.)
supermarket supermercato (m.)
supper cena (f.)
to support (sports) fare il tifo per
supporter, fan tifoso
sure certo, sicuro
surname cognome (m.)
sweater maglione (m.)
to swim nuotare
swimming pool piscina (f.)
system sistema (m.)

to take préndere
to take back portare di ritorno
tall alto
to taste assaggiare
taxi taxi (m.)
teacher insegnante (m. & f.)
telegramme telegramma (m.)
telephone teléfono (m.)
television televisione (f.)
temperature febbre (f.)
ten dieci
tenor tenore (m.)

tent tenda (f.)
terrace terrazzo (m.)
thank goodness meno male
thank you grazie
that che
that is (i.e.) cioè
that which ciò che, quello che
the il (m.), la (f.)
theatre teatro (m.)
then allora, dunque, poi
there li
thesis tesi (f.)
thing cosa (f.)
things roba (f.)
to think crédere, pensare
thirst sete (f.)
thirteen trédici
thirty trenta
this questo
this morning stamattina
thousand mille
three tre
Thursday giovedì (m.)
ticket biglietto (m.)
tie cravatta (f.)
time volta (f.)
timetable orario (m.)
tip mancia (m.)
tired stanco
to get tired stancarsi
to a
tobacconist tabaccaio/a
today oggi
toe dito (m.)
together with insieme a
toilet gabinetto (m.)
tomato pomodoro (m.)
tomorrow domani
tonight stasera
too anche
too much, too troppo
top cima (f.)
tourist tax tassa di soggiorno (f.)
town città (f.)
trade union sindacato (m.)
traffic tráffico (m.)

tragic trágico
train treno (m.)
transport trasporto (m.)
to travel viaggiare
trip gita (f.)
trout trota (f.)
true vero
truth verità (f.)
Tuesday martedì (m.)
twelve dódici
twenty venti
two due

ugly brutto
unbeatable insuperábile
uncle zio (m.)
under sotto
underground metropolitana (f.)
to understand capire, inténdere
unfortunately purtroppo
uniform divisa (f.)
unique unico
university università (f.)
until finchè … non, fino...a
unwell indisposto
to use usare

vacuum cleaner aspirapólvere (m.)
valid válido
veal vitello (m.)
veal cutlet cotoletta (f.)
vegetable verdura (f.)
vegetarian vegetariano
Venice Venezia (f.)
very molto
very bad péssimo
very well beníssimo
violinist violinista (m. & f.)
visit visita (f.)
to visit (person) andare a trovare
to visit (place) visitare
voice voce (f.)
vote voto (m.)
to vote votare
voucher buono (m.)
to wait aspettare, atténdere

waiter cameriere (m.)
walk passeggiata, camminata (f.)
to walk camminare
to want volere
to warn avvisare
washing machine lavatrice (f.)
to wash oneself lavarsi
watchmaker orologiaio/a
water acqua (f.)
way senso (m.)
to wear portare
Wednesday mercoledì (m.)
week settimana (f.)
welcome benvenuto
west ovest (m.)
what che, che cosa
whatever qualsíasi,
  qualunque
when quando
where dove
where from di dove
which quale, che
white bianco
who? chi
who, whom che, il quale, cui
why perchè, come mai
wife moglie (f.)

willingly volentieri
window finestra (f.)
winter inverno (m.)
wish voglia
to wish desiderare
with con
wood legno (m.)
world mondo (m.)
worried preoccupato
to worry preoccuparsi
worse peggiore
worse (adv.) peggio
to write scrívere
wrong sbagliato, torto

year anno
yes sì
yes (certainly!) come no!
yesterday ieri
yet ancora
you tu, Lei, voi
young gióvane
younger, youngest minore

zero zero (m.)
zip cerniera (f.)
zoo zoo (m.)

Index

Items are cross-referred to numbered sections unless a specific page or Week dialogue is shown.